Beginnings

in Jewish

philosophy

The

Jewish

Heritage

Series

Beginnings in Jewish philosophy

MEYER LEVIN

Behrman House, Inc. *Publishers*

NEW YORK, N.Y.

With fullest appreciation and gratitude, I wish to acknowledge the unstinting guidance of Rabbi Eugene B. Borowitz in the planning and formation of this book.

I also acknowledge the help of Rabbi Morrison D. Bial, Rabbi David Gordis and Mr. Matthew Mosenkis for their critical evaluations; and Cilli Brandstatter for the research.

DESIGNED BY BETTY BINNS

Manufactured in the United States of America
Library of Congress Catalog Card Number: 76-116677
Standard Book Number: 87441-063-0

Contents

INTRODUCTION: You and Judaism

What does it mean to you to be a Jew? That is, as you reach the age of religious responsibility, and prepare to take your place in the Jewish—and the world—communities, what beliefs do you share with other Jews? What, as a Jew, will you be expected to believe?

Now no one who has reached the age of reason can be told what to believe. That would be a contradiction in terms, and Judaism recognizes this. You will find that it offers basic guidelines which have come down to us through revelation, inspiration, and past experience. You will want to be aware of these and to consider their meaning and promise. You will also find in Judaism much freedom for individual interpretation and application of basic ideas.

Asking questions

You will find, too, that there is plenty of room in Judaism for raising questions. In each generation, young people reach the stage of questioning the knowledge and rules of their elders. Furthermore, you yourselves happen to live in a time when much of mankind finds itself questioning the knowledge and rules—and ideas—inherited from the past. How adequate have they proved? Have they failed us? Have they perhaps been mis-applied? Or insufficiently applied? Or, in some areas, not applied at all? Were they in themselves mistaken, or well-founded?

Searching for answers

It is important for us to question, and to find answers—as far as possible. When very young children ask questions beyond their years, they are frequently told, "that is something you will understand when you are older." You may have had that experience yourself when you were in the early grades. And you have probably found that the promise has been kept, to some extent at least. You have already had answers to some of the questions that you raised when you were younger. But you may also have found that for the deepest questions there are no complete answers.

Still, we keep trying to find answers—in many fields. In the academic world knowledge has been changing so fast that you as a member of a new generation have been given answers, and techniques in problem-solving, that are new to your parents. Many of these are actually new applications or extensions of old knowledge. In mathematics, for instance, one used to be taught simply that two times two make four. And we know that it still does *if* one is using the old familiar one-ten-one hundred place system. But today's mathematics is geared to the computer age. One uses the multiplication table in terms of the place system employed in a given problem. But the principle of multiplication has not changed. The table is still valid.

Similar changes are taking place in many fields of learning. Discoveries go forward, but they also reach backward. New words, new signs are invented to explain new dis-coveries, and then these new words have to be put back to the very start of our edu-cation so that we can harmonize the old, beginning knowledge with the new.

Old and new ideas

The same is true of the greatest subject that faces mankind, the question of God. As we make more and more discoveries about space, about the atom, about the way life begins, our religious thinkers reach back to the very beginning of religion to harmonize what was already generally understood with what is being scientifically uncovered.

At times there appears to be contradiction instead of harmony. And there are people who become convinced that new discoveries prove certain old ideas to be wrong.

This harmonizing of new and old knowl-edge involves thinking for yourself, judging for yourself between different ideas that are put before you. We are not simply going to say, "You must believe thus and so because it has been decided for you," but we are going to say, "Here are different ideas. De-cide for yourself which you can accept."

In this book we are going to try to show

you how one system of beliefs, Judaism, has grown through this process. These ideas need not be final decisions for you. You must keep your mind open, for later on you may find new material, or you may grow into a new way of thinking that changes your answers. But it is already a great step to come to the point where you are not asked to take important things for granted.

Limits to knowledge

There is still another step. This is when people admit that they do not know the answers to certain questions. Not because they have forgotten the algebra they learned in school, or have not learned the new math or the names of new nations that have only recently come into being. People may not know the answers to such factual questions offhand, but they know where to look up the answers.

There is a greater kind of "don't know." This "don't know" applies to questions that are unanswerable. And it is also a turning point in life, when we first face—and admit to ourselves—that there are things that cannot be known.

Although you are not yet fully mature, you are now old enough to know the simple truth that even the great scientists, even the rabbis and the greatest religious thinkers of all time, cannot know all the answers to the question of God. Some thinkers even define God as That Which We Do Not Know.

We are told that some prophets heard or received the words of God. There are vari-ous ways of understanding this. We will talk and think about them. For now we have come to the point of looking beyond the easier answers given to childhood; now you are more free to think for yourself. But you must have material to think from, and think about, and we will try to set that material before you.

An open religion

In these studies you will be thinking about Judaism. Our point of view is that Judaism is an open religion.

Now this itself is a point about which you can have some hot arguments. You already know that there are religions with a closed, or fixed, system of beliefs. Such beliefs are called *dogmas*. They must be accepted to start with. When a person sticks to his beliefs in spite of any contradictory facts you can produce, he is called *dogmatic*. But a dogma may also prove to be true.

Here are a few examples of dogma from various religions:

> The belief that there is an actual heaven, an actual hell.
>
> The belief that people are reincarnated.
>
> The belief that God had a Son on earth.
>
> The belief that God is One.

The last is a belief shared by the great religions of our time. In some, it is part of a system of dogmas. In Judaism it is the only dogma, or as we see it, the only belief of which we are certain and without which there can be no religion.

There have been Jews who believed dogmatically in many other ideas. There are good religious Jews who believe in reincarnation. There are also good religious Jews who do not. In spite of many myths and sayings in this regard, it remains an open question. The same is true of heaven and hell. But these are not dogmas in Judaism, either on the yes or the no side.

There are Jews who have many other absolute beliefs and who insist that any of us who leave out their beliefs are not really religious Jews. Yet there is no supreme center of authority in Judaism to back them up or to back up those who believe differently. There is a vast collection of laws, of rules, of advice, of traditions, of wisdom, and out of this Judaism proceeds.

How can we all have the same faith, Judaism, if some believe there is a heaven, if some believe souls are born anew, if some believe in actual miracles, and others do not?

That is what we mean by an open religion. We see Judaism as a growing and changing and developing way of seeking God. We use the entire history of our way of thinking and feeling about God to continue our search. Some people even say that an open religion includes Jews who do not believe there is a God. Even these people may be defended if they are not dogmatic in their atheism and if they accept the moral intuitions that have guided us as a people, for they simply may not want to accept the word God.

A pattern of worship

But of course Judaism does not accept and include all religious points of view, because then it would cease to be a way in itself. Judaism does not accept the dogmas of other religions or their ways of worship. While Judaism may be the basic faith of someone who rarely or never enters a synagogue, it does include a whole pattern of worship.

All of us take part in testing, examining, renewing, our belief and our ways of worship. To do this honestly and fruitfully we must know as much as we can about how Judaism grew, we must know of the different ideas that have been accepted, changed, given up, or seen in a new light. And this book is intended to supply some of that material, to send you to look for more material, to open the way for your own thinking about, and contribution to, the function of Jewish values in your life.

The world we live in

1 Who made the world?

It is the mystery of life itself that first awakens in us the feeling of awe and wonder that goes beyond any other feeling. Our need to express this leads to religious worship.

And then, filled with that same sense of wonder and awe of life, we want to know best how to use this life, how to choose actions that satisfy our sense of right and wrong, good and bad. And we reach out to the God of the Scriptures, who said, at the beginning of creation, "Let there be light."

Each child, before being taught religion, may "make up" for himself some imaginary answers to the mystery of creation. He begins the way the early human beings, the primitives, began, with magical notions, or he begins by telling himself that God is in the sun, or in the moon, or in a secret place in the forest, or a deep mysterious cave, or an ancient tree, or in the wind.

From such ideas, with the help of teaching, he grows to the idea of a single source of creation, a bodiless spiritual identity. Thus in a few years each child of today may go through the early evolution of religious thinking, a social process that took mankind several thousand years.

But even this process was short compared

to the thousands upon thousands of years of the biological evolution of mankind. Scientists tell us that in our bodies, before we are born, the entire course of evolution is repeated in the space of only a few months; we pass through the stages of animal life, from creatures of the sea to human form. This same evolutionary idea can be used to study society. Each person, usually early in life, may pass from a stage of magical beliefs to present-day religious forms. Most of us never quite give up all of those magical beliefs, keeping vestiges of them, just as our bodies keep vestiges of earlier stages in evolution.

Science and religion

While religion grows from our awe and wonder at life, science grows by learning to explain some of life's wonders. Therefore, some people feel that science is replacing religion, and they themselves cease to have any religious belief. On the other hand, many highly advanced scientists are deeply religious. The greatest scientists are the first to affirm that the more they learn of the structure of the universe, the more in awe they feel of creation itself. So that man's first religious impulse, to worship creation, is not denied but affirmed by science. And the second impulse, to develop our spiritual sense of how to live, how to do what is right, is not touched upon by physical science at all.

We all know that some people object to religion on the grounds that science disproves the story of creation in the Bible. And we all know certain answers, first that the idea of a "day" in the creation story may be

One of the most awesome—and most beautiful—sights in nature is the Grand Canyon cut by the Colorado River. The oldest of its many colored layers dates back to early Pre-Cambrian times when only simple forms of life existed on our earth.

taken to mean a space of time, even an aeon. And that a series of days of creation could mean aeons of evolution, from chaos, to an atmosphere, to a mass of matter, to the separation of the seas from dry land, and so on. Even an Orthodox person can accept, without a feeling of conflict, modern scientific explanations of how the world evolved through aeons of time. Many, of course, cannot and do not accept this.

Among Jews there is an anecdote about "a day in God's sight," which may mean millions of years by human measurement. A poor man prays to God, "Dear God, if I only had a thousand dollars I could go into business. Let me have it. To You it is just a penny." God answers, "I'll help you. But wait a minute."

It's a typically Jewish way of making us understand an idea, by salting it with a moral warning—this time against an exaggerated sense of self-importance.

There is another way of thinking about the relations between religion and science. Isn't it rather artful to try to make every word of the Bible fit what scientists discover? Instead of trying to translate advanced science back into the Biblical language of more than three thousand years ago, isn't it better to try to put ourselves in the place of our ancestors, to identify with them, and then to follow the course of Judaism as it evolved from their early understanding?

Stories of creation

We know today, from world-wide studies of ancient myths and beliefs, that our Biblical story of creation was not the only one of its kind. It was an imaginative and intuitive explanation, similar to some of the explanations offered by other peoples. Yet our Bible contains the germs of important ideas not found in other creation stories. Just about every people on earth has its creation tales: some are poetic, as are those of various American Indian tribes; some are very complicated, and some are pretty wild. These stories make fascinating reading, and you can find them in books dealing with anthropology.

The tales that are closest to the Biblical account come, as you would expect, from the part of the world that Abraham came from. They are the oldest human writings so far discovered. These Bible-like creation stories have been deciphered from writings on stones found in Mesopotamia, the general area of what we today call Iraq, that was in Biblical times named Babylonia, and before that called Akkadia. It is the "Garden of Eden" region between the two great rivers, the Tigris and the Euphrates.

In this area people were called Sumerians, and in their legends is a garden called Eden, with a serpent and a tree of life. But the Bible adds a moral: that by eating of the forbidden fruit from the Tree of Knowledge, man learned about good and evil and thus became responsible to choose between them. And there are other significant differences between the Akkadian and the Biblical stories.

The Akkadian creation epic begins with the words, "When on high," or *Enuman Elish,* and is known by that name. Like our own Genesis story, it tells how creation was

Eve is shown, on this pewter plate, offering the forbidden fruit to Adam. Behind them you can spy the serpent entwined in the sinuous branches of the tree.

the act of bringing order and life out of chaos. Like our Genesis story, it tells of steps in the act of creation, first light, then the firmament, then the earth, the sun, moon, and stars, then birds and fish and great sea monsters, and finally, man.

But in the Akkadian myth these deeds of creation are accomplished by many gods, and on the seventh day they hold a feast and exalt Marduk as their chief. In the Bible a great step is made from this primitive explanation toward a moral and spiritual conception. The Bible tells of one impulse only, one God, and after each act of creation God sees that what He has made "is good." A spirit of moral value has come into the creation story. This meaning is in that word *good.* And on the seventh day, the Creator rests.

Some see, in the order of creation as it is given in these myths, the birth of the understanding of evolution. The science of the cosmos too has a theory of the universe being formed in stages, out of chaos, until the beginning of life takes place in the sea, and continues to the creation of man. In Judaism, we are free to speculate over such points. There are scholars who wonder whether the similarity of various creation legends is a result of ancient man's observation and intuitive understanding of nature, whether it is, indeed, a guess toward the theory of evolution. So powerful is the need for understanding that some people even imagine the story goes far, far back to some mysterious time when the truth of creation was known to mankind, and that in some way it became obliterated from the mind of man.

Stories of the flood

There is another, later, legend found to be repeated in many cultures about this very question, the obliteration of all the works of man. That is the deluge story. Again, the closest account to the one in the Bible comes from Abraham's region. It is called the Gilgamesh epic. Telling of the quest of a young man, Gilgamesh, for the secret of life, this epic describes a flood and the building of an ark:

Man of Shurupak, son of Ubar-tutu,
Tear down (this) house, build a ship!
Give up possessions, seek thou life.
Foreswear (worldly) goods, and keep thy soul
  alive!
Aboard the ship take thou the seed of all living
  things.
The ship that thou shalt build,
Her dimensions shall be to measure . . .

And similarly the Bible tells us,

And God said to Noah, "The time has come for the end of all flesh, because they have filled the earth with corruption and violence. Therefore make yourself an ark of gopher wood, and make rooms in the ark, and cover it inside and out with pitch."

The dimensions of the ark are given and then Noah is told,

. . . and you shall enter the ark, you and your sons and your wife, and your sons' wives with you. And of every living thing, two of every sort, male and female, shall you bring into the ark to keep them alive with you; . . .

The appearance of the flood story in other parts of the world has made people wonder whether there really was such a universal deluge, or did various parts of the world, even at different periods, suffer from tidal floods, so that the "whole world," as far as the people in each place knew of it, seemed to be covered with water? In this way the same myth could have been born in widely separated places.

The Bible—anthology with a difference

The Bible story of the flood differs from others in that it draws a moral, just as the Bible story of creation draws a moral. The Bible constantly draws morals from whatever knowledge of the world men had or imagined they had. From the world they saw around them, from the myths handed down since time immemorial, the wise men of old began to explain that there was order in creation, harmony, beauty, purpose. This is what the ancient sages meant when they said God saw that what He had made was good.

As scientific knowledge increased, man came to know that he was not made like a sculpture out of clay but that human beings have developed, probably over the last half million years. Today we stand on the threshold of discovering about life on other planets and perhaps even of creating living matter in test tubes. Yet all this does not affect the poetic interpretations and spiritual teaching of the Bible.

The Bible is a gathering together, a collection like a vast anthology, of works written across a period of about twelve hundred years. Some of these writings put down what had even then already been passed along verbally for thousands of years before. These ancient sayings, which became writings, dealt with cosmology and the creation of life. Later on, the Bible stories dealt with actual history, and much of this history has been proved quite exact by archeological digs in recent times. The writings also contained moral tales, visions, laws, and poems.

Impact of Judaism

The growth of moral understanding among the Jews inspired two other major religions, Christianity and Islam, the faith of the Muslims. Both spring from Judaism. Thus, half of the world today believes in systems of morality inspired by Judaism. Meanwhile Judaism itself has never ceased developing and has never, for Jews, lost its supreme validity.

The people who believed in Marduk and his lesser gods have been lost to history and their religion is a relic. In these same lands of Akkadia today live mostly Muslims, or Moslems, as they are popularly called. The Greek religion, thriving in the days of the Jewish Temple, is only a collection of tales to the Greeks of today, who are mostly Christians. The people of Egypt, who in those early times had an elaborate religion with many mythological gods, today are almost all Muslims, though they also have an extensive Christian sect called Coptic.

Judaism and science

Judaism has continued for the very reason that it is not a frozen, dogmatic set of beliefs, but a system of moral discovery that constantly refers back to all we know from the past. It has no basic conflict with science because it is concerned with spiritual and moral values. If the physical sciences test and measure the way in which the world is made, Judaism tests the way in which man makes his life decisions.

In the end, it is true, there is a dream, a hope, of a final fusion between the spiritual and the material life, a time when the very innermost secret of life, the mystery of creation, may be revealed, and a time in which the physical world may be seen as merging itself with a divine moral purpose.

But today, despite the strides of science in the last fifty years, advances that go beyond what was learned in all the thousands of years before, we still have made little spiritual progress beyond what was revealed to our prophets in Biblical times. Many feel that when we read in the Bible of God speaking to Abraham, to Moses, to Isaiah, we are reading of a time when there was less of a cloud between man and the divine impulse, and that indeed these prophets of old understood divinity much more clearly than we do today. That is one of the reasons that we study and cherish their words and build on their insight.

Scientists and philosophers describe the differences between science and religion, but also the common impulses. Alfred North

Whitehead, in *Science and the Modern World,* says:

The *conflict* between religion and science is what naturally comes to our minds when we think of this subject. It seems as though, during the last half century, the results of science and the beliefs of religion had come into a position of frank disagreement, from which there can be no escape, except by abandoning either the clear teaching of science, or the clear teaching of religion . . . Religion is the vision of something which stands beyond, behind, and within, the passing flux of immediate things; something which is real, and yet waiting to be realized; something which is a remote possibility, and yet the greatest of present facts; something that gives meaning to all that passes, and yet eludes apprehension; something whose possession is the final good, and yet is beyond all reach; something which is the ultimate ideal, and the hopeless quest.

Let us suppose that the Bible were written today and that men of science contributed the stories of creation. The details would of course be quite different. But the moral principle would remain unchanged. Where science seems to conflict with the Bible or revealed religion, it is because the Bible has used examples from the limited knowledge of the physical world, the knowledge of the men of earlier times. But the spiritual knowledge of those men was advanced.

Albert Einstein said that science without religion is lame; and religion without science is blind. Do not fear to question and to question scientifically. The eternal question is part of Judaism.

Bible stories have made their way into the culture of many lands. This illustration from an Arabic manuscript (1306 c.e.) shows Jonah seated under the miraculous gourd (Jonah 4). It also recalls his earlier adventure with the great fish (Jonah 1 and 2).

2 Are there really miracles?

When men beheld order in the universe, in the rising and setting of the sun, the movement of the stars, they were in awe of creation and believed in God because of this perfect and beautiful orderliness. Today, as science discovers the vast and minute complexity that regulates creation, we feel just as deeply the presence of the divine power. But does this divine power intervene in the affairs of men by sometimes changing the order of nature?

Order of intervention

Einstein said, "I believe in Spinoza's God, who reveals Himself in the harmony of all being, not in a god who concerns Himself with the fate and actions of men."

But the ancients, who already saw God in the perfection of nature, saw another proof of God when the order of nature seemed to be broken. And to them, this was an even stronger proof of God. Such a happening, called a *miracle*, meant that God was aware, was watching, and would intervene to help the good people, or the ones who believed in Him even if the laws of nature had to be broken or interrupted.

We still debate the existence of miracles. There are people who believe in them exactly as they are related in the Bible or in other religious works. Others seek a natural explanation, but say that the event, coming at the instant it was needed, was still a miraculous happening. On the opposite side are people who do not believe in religion, they say, because they cannot believe in miracles. But for the Jewish faith, belief in miracles does not decide whether or not a person is religious.

Our changing beliefs

Thinking about miracles can help us to understand the growth and changes in our own people's idea of God. First, we ask, why did so many people in ancient times need a miracle to prove to them the existence and power of God? As if life itself, the universe itself, were not proof! The miracle is offered to show that He who can make the sun can also make the sun stop—like someone holding back the hand of a clock, and then setting it in motion again. This idea of the miracle as proof of God may today be seen as rather childish. It is also anthropomorphic; that is, it follows man's early way of imagining God in human terms, except far grander.

Yet such proof of God is still offered today. It is as though God were some sort of supermagician who had to prove himself by doing the seemingly impossible. We lose faith in the magician when we understand how he manages his tricks; so people whose faith depends on miracles are in danger of losing their faith when a natural explanation for a miracle is produced.

Oddly enough, people who have a higher, or more abstract, sense of God, feel a kind of satisfaction when a natural explanation of

The architectural strength and graceful delicate pattern of a spider web present a miracle of beauty to the beholder— and of utility to the spider.

a miracle is produced, for it detaches God from these magical connections.

The search for natural explanations

There are all sorts of natural explanations offered for the miracles spoken of in the Bible. Such explanations need not destroy the faith of a believer in miracles, for he can answer, "Of course God used natural means to produce the miracle. He sent a wind to divide the Red Sea (or the Sea of Reeds, as it is in the original text). But the wind came just at that crucial moment so as to help the Jews to cross, and stopped at the next moment, to drown the Egyptian pursuers."

Thus, a direct intervention, even if it is explained through nature, is still seen as a miracle. God is supposed to take sides. Almost every army has had a battle cry, such as "God is with us." But then we ask, if there are good people and bad people on both sides, why should the good people among the Egyptian soldiers be destroyed with the bad, in order to save the bad Jews among the good?

Then what did happen, in the events called miracles? Let us see if we can follow through the way in which a miracle story might develop.

One of the most common types of miracle stories is that about the sign sent from heaven to convince those who doubt God's power. Such a story is the one about the miraculous fire that struck the altar of Elijah, while a doubting crowd saw that no fire came down to light the altar of the rival priests. The story of Moses and the burning bush is also a story of a sign given to a doubter. Moses saw a dry thorny bush on fire, yet the bush was not consumed. The voice of God came to him from the bush, commanding him to return to Egypt and bring the Jews out from slavery to freedom.

We can point to far-out explanations offered for these supernatural events. One whole group of explainers believes in trickiness. Elijah, they say, must have known about the oily wastes of the Dead Sea region and used oil on his wood. As for Moses, the "natural" school of explainers tells us that there is indeed a bush that grows in dry, desert areas, including the area where Moses tended his sheep. And this plant secretes a compound that forms a gas around the bush; this gas can ignite, without burning the bush itself. Moses might have come upon this phenomenon for the first time, and might at that very moment have been thinking about the plight of the Jews in Egypt and feeling guilty at having deserted them. The intensity of his emotion, the seeming miracle of the bush—and there is your explanation.

Origins of miracle stories

But if we want to be rational we can provide still a further explanation. We can ask, how did this story come to us? Through telling and retelling, until it was finally written down.

Or perhaps Moses himself told of a moment of inner struggle, of doubt, of contemplation, when he happened on the burning

The story of the Exodus and its leader grips the minds of men. This painting of Moses and Aaron with the Ten Commandments was made by a seventeenth-century Flemish artist.

bush. This time the awesome sight appeared as a symbol to him: Go and do the dangerous thing that burns in your mind. You see by this fire that you will not necessarily be destroyed.

In this way we can, if we wish, try to explain and interpret the physical facts of many miracles. It is interesting that Judaism speaks less and less about miracles as time goes on, even though Judaism keeps growing as a faith. There are miracle-tales of Elijah and Elisha, but none in the words of Isaiah, Jeremiah, and Hosea. It is important to notice that there is no such thing as "authentication" of miracles in Judaism by a theological body, as there is in other religions such as Christianity.

Man's longing for miracles

People of all faiths wish for miracles to happen, to help them. Most commonly this deep wish is expressed over a serious or incurable illness. And so people will journey to shrines of saints, to whom they pray, for intervention with God.

Lourdes, in France, is such a shrine for Christians, in memory of a farm girl who saw visions and became a saint. The Cave of Elijah, in Israel, is visited by Jews who ask for help of all kinds, including healing. And every year at Lag B'Omer thousands of pilgrims gather at Meron, at the tombs of the ancient Rabbis, to drop in notes, asking for cures and miracles.

There are often "proofs" of such healing; those who believe in miracles say they are "from God," and nationalists say that under intense emotion changes can take place in the body.

A strong revival of the Jewish folk belief in miracles came with the rise of the Ḥasidic movement a few hundred years ago, first among simple Jews in the remote villages of the Carpathian Mountains, and then throughout Poland and the Ukraine. The originator of the movement, Rabbi Israel, the Baal Shem Tov, is even called the "wonder rabbi." He brings children to the childless; he makes a week's journey to Berlin overnight, by horse and wagon. All these wondrous stories are taken by scholars who do not believe in miracles as evidence of the Baal Shem's effect on his followers, as signs of his profound personality. Instead of miracles, many Jews seek in Ḥasidism its renewal of a direct sense of spiritual contact with God.

Modern miracle tales

Yet the sense of the miraculous lives in all of us and is really a part of our spiritual feeling, our sense that all creation and all life is on a higher level than what our brain understands. We often speak of being "saved by a miracle," as when a car skids and overturns, and no one is hurt. Or we have examples from recent events in Israel that might well give rise to miracle stories like those in the Bible.

An elderly settler, Yehoshua Brandstatter, telling of the days when Jewish villages were few and far between, recalls an incident from half a century ago. Yehoshua had

The flag of Israel with the Star of David flies in a free land, refreshing the sense of miracle in our time. Here Israeli youth carry it in Jerusalem, celebrating the anniversary of Israel's Independence.

then owned a beautiful gray mare, so famous in the region that he himself was called, not by his own name, but Abu Sarga, which means the Master of the Gray. One day while Yehoshua and a comrade were riding along a wadi, they were attacked by a band of marauders who were after the celebrated horse. Yehoshua's friend galloped to their village for help, while the Master of the Gray held off the band of attackers with only his pistol. Suddenly, as if at a signal, they all turned and fled! The settlers puzzled over this. But the next day an ancient, wrinkled Arab passed by the Jewish village and explained what had happened. The story told by the marauders was that all at once they had seen angels hovering around the head of Abu Sarga, protecting him from their hail of bullets. And so they had taken off!

Who knows what they saw.

The Israel War of Independence gave rise to numbers of miracle tales that, three thousand years ago, might have rivaled what happened in the campaigns of Joshua. The very fact that a small, poorly armed nation held off seven armies representing forty times its own population appeared as a miracle. And within this miraculous situation were wondrous tales. There is the story of Yoḥai ben Nun, who volunteered on a suicidal mission. He was to ride a torpedo, so as to aim it at an Egyptian destroyer. Since Israel then had no navy, a rowboat carried Yoḥai within a few miles of the warship. The torpedo was launched, with Yoḥai astride. Revolving searchlights from the Egyptian ship were scanning the sea, and by every reasonable calculation they would be certain to pick out the manned missile. Their machine guns would kill the rider, but too late to keep the pointed torpedo from reaching its target.

Suddenly, while Yoḥai's comrades watched his suicide attack, the searchlight beams vanished, all was black, and there came the reverberation of the explosion. Silently, Yoḥai's friends watched the blazing enemy ship, their exultation subdued by their thoughts of their heroic comrade. They turned and began to row away, when a half-drowned howl reached their ears. Frantically they headed for the sound. Yoḥai ben Nun appeared at the boatside, like a spirit risen from the sea.

What had happened? As by a miracle, he said, the Egyptian searchlights had gone completely dark just as he got near enough to aim his torpedo and leap off. Yoḥai ben Nun lived to become the first admiral of the Israeli navy.

Should it be written that the hand of God came down and cast darkness upon the waters, to save the life of the future admiral?

Where, then, do we stand on miracles?

Teachings of the Talmud

While stories of miracles are told in connection with the Jewish religion, the Talmud expressly forbids Jews to "rely on miracles." We must face our problems; we must use our teachings to help us solve each situation according to what is right and just, but we must not wait for a miracle to help us or to save us.

Jewish thinkers in medieval times would not accept claimed miracles as proof of the righteousness of Jewish beliefs. The famous scholar Gersonides, Levi ben Gerson, said, "If natural phenomena and laws were changed by miracles . . . it would signify the defeat of the natural order. . . . In plane geometry, no miracle could produce a triangle the sum of whose angles are less than two right angles, nor is it possible by a miracle today to cause rain not to have fallen in Jerusalem yesterday when as a matter of fact it did fall."

Modern views

In modern times, the usual view is to explain miracles as natural happenings, coincidences which the ancients could not understand. But there are leaders in Judaism who go further and regard miracle stories as harmful because they keep up the spirit of superstition and prevent some people from thinking more deeply about their religion. The leader of the Reconstructionist movement, Dr. Mordecai Kaplan, followed this view, and so all "signs and wonders" have been taken out of the Reconstructionist prayer book.

As we would expect, miracles provide a ground for argument between science and religion. Still, in the spiritual realm, we can see many everyday miracles, or events that would seem like miracles from a materialist's point of view. There are miracles of restored faith and courage, after wildernesses of doubt and disappointment. There is the miracle of forgiving, where strict rea-

son might make hate and bitterness more lasting. There is the miracle of regeneration when men have turned again from wrong ways—perhaps led into them through injustice in their own lives—and renewed once more, in obedience, their Jewish sense of partnership with God. All these, and many more, are "miracles" strictly in accordance with the Law.

A search for meaning

This view does not mean that the scientific mind simply dismisses all accounts of miracles. Today, science looks to myths, legends, and ancient belief for clues to understanding the mysterious and even contradictory workings in the order of nature. The areas of hypnosis, telepathy, and clairvoyance are studied. Even the phenomenon called *telekinesis*, the movement of objects without their being touched, is being scientifically examined.

Discoveries still to come in these fields will surely give us more explanations of what were called miracles in the old days. But none of this changes the deeper question connected with miracles, the question of the direct interference of God in a human situation.

Modern Jewish thinkers would rather see it this way: a godly person, one who strongly feels the divine impulse toward doing what is good, rises to unusual perceptions and actions in times of great stress. That is what Moses did. That is what the prophets did, who cried out the Word of the Lord. That is the miracle from within ourselves.

UNIT TWO

How Judaism
learned about
our world

3 The Judaism of Abraham, Isaac, and Jacob

Does your mother or your sister wear a charm bracelet? Or perhaps, if a girl, you yourself have one? There will be all sorts of little images, fish, birds, animals, or tokens like a heart, a key, a Jewish star, dangling from this bracelet. Half-seriously, you may say these are good luck charms. Each may stand for one kind of luck, in health, in love, in riches.

Vestiges of paganism

The charm bracelet is a vestige of pagan worship, of the amulets worn in all societies; these personal charms are like the little household gods that each family kept sacred. In the Bible, the little family gods were called *terafim*. The *terafim* were part of the whole system of gods, or *baalim*, great and small, in many an ancient civilization.

We do not take our good luck gods very seriously today. But some very sophisticated people can get upset if a favorite charm is lost or broken. Mostly we smile over these superstitions as among the whimsies of women, but men too can take their good luck amulets very much to heart. Ernest Hemingway, we learn from a friend and biographer, always had to have a good luck charm with him, and once when Mr. Hemingway lost his charm he became seriously depressed. His friend had instantly to give him a replacement, anything at all, so as not to leave him "unprotected."

Ancient superstitions

If modern man still refuses to break completely from ancient beliefs, how difficult must this have been for those who did make the first break with superstition! We can, in the Bible, watch this struggle taking place among our patriarchs and their families, and going down to the time of Moses and the golden calf. And even today you might see that golden calf as a miniature bull's head dangling from a bracelet.

While we could read about the *terafim* in the Bible, more recently archaeologists have put into our hands those very same little clay household gods. Samples may be seen in almost any museum. Copies of such gods, from many cultures—Canaanite, Greek, Roman, African, Indian, Mexican—can be bought at modest prices. Even originals, the actual ancient bits of bronze or clay, can be bought for only a few dollars, so abundantly have they been dug up.

It is the ones from Canaan—now Israel—and from Mesopotamia, that are most interesting; they show how real was the religious problem of Abraham and his offspring.

Beginning of Judaism

We know that Judaism had to develop over many centuries before there was such a placc as a synagogue. But we tend to forget that in the time of the patriarchs there was little more than a stone altar, that, and a basic religious idea. Did Abraham have prayers to recite? Did he have a Sabbath? Did he have a definite ritual, and a place of worship? Did he have kosher laws? Were his rules of justice the same as ours? Were his marriage laws like those of today's Orthodox Jews?

Some of these questions we can, in whole or in part, answer. We know that when Abraham sought a bride for his son Isaac, he sent for a girl from his own tribe. And we know of one most important event: that he had a covenant with the Lord, a vision, a promise that he would be favored, blessed, and would receive the lands that lay before him for his family and his seed forever. The sign of this covenant between God and Abraham was circumcision.

Did this custom begin with Abraham or were there tribes that practiced circumcision, perhaps without attaching the rite to the idea of a covenant? We know that circumcision has been widely practiced on various continents; an ancient clay figure from Mesopotamia shows a man who definitely appears to be circumcised.

The world of Abraham

We begin to see Abraham as emerging from a certain culture that he carries with him, at least in part, to a different land. Excavations have shown us a good deal about that culture as it existed in Abraham's land of birth, some four thousand years ago.

Two great excavations, at Ugarit and Mari, must be thought about, as well as the famous excavation at the city of Ur itself. Numerous tablets found in these places help us to understand some of the passages and the place names in the Bible, for both the Hebrew and Ugarit tongues come from the same source, a Canaanite language.

Mari was close to Ur, on the banks of the Euphrates, and was one of the ten great cities of ancient Mesopotamia. It was the capital of the Mari kingdom which was destroyed about 1750 B.C.E.

The land and the city of Haran, where Abraham lived, were probably under Mari control, and the very names of people in his family appear on the ancient Mari tablets. In the valley of Haran even today there is a place which is called Terah—the name of Abraham's father.

Some twenty thousand inscribed tablets were found in Mari, and many have yet to be deciphered. Already they have given us much information about the customs, laws, and ways of life of Abraham's neighbors. There is a letter about a tribe causing trouble to the last king of the Maris, Zimri-um; the name of the marauding tribe is B'nei Yamin. And in Genesis (49:27) we also read of a troublesome tribe, "Benjamin is a marauding wolf. . . ."

Journey to freedom

Such touches show us that Abraham and his clan were real personalities, living in the social framework of their times. Then, we are told, Abraham decided to seek a land where he could worship more freely. Why?

The ruins of ancient Ur lie desolate under a glaring sun. But archaeologists have found in them traces of a high civilization in Abraham's time.

In Abraham's area there was a rigid form of idol worship, a state church. Abraham's inspiration, his sense of the unity of God, caused him to leave, seeking freedom of conscience, freedom of worship. Where could he go? In the neighboring land of Canaan, idol worship was also prevalent. But it seems that the social structure was not so tightly organized in Canaan. There was no church-state. Instead, there were fortified towns, each with its "king," so that this newcomer, wandering between the forts with his clan, was free to abstain from Canaanite worship.

Struggles with paganism

Yet the newcomers, called Hebrews, did not keep themselves entirely closed off from the local tribes, for we see them adopting a Canaanite language. Even the word for God, though not His Name (which was mysterious, and not to be uttered), came from the Canaanites. Among their deities was a powerful storm god, Ba'al, and *baal* became a Hebrew word for god. It means master and is also used for head of the house, *baal ha-bayit,* and for husband, and for owner. The chief god of all among the Canaanites was called El, and El became the Hebrew designation for God, sometimes called *El-elyon*, the Highest.

If there was a highest, were there also lower gods, even among Abraham's folk? If people cling to charms, amulets, and idols today, could Abraham's folk have discarded them?

We read how Abraham's grandson, Jacob,

married a kinswoman, Rachel, in the household of Laban in their old country of Haran. And we read how the *terafim* were so important that Rachel stole them to take away with her, when she and Jacob left her father's household. Jacob finally had to insist that all these little gods be buried in the ground, under the tree at Shechem (Gen. 35:4). We can almost hear him shouting, "An end to all this superstition!"

We read how Abraham himself struggled against a grievous custom of the neighboring tribes, the rite of human sacrifice. He went as far as placing his son Isaac on the altar. And the story then tells us that he was ordered by God to substitute a ram. Perhaps this whole story was a teaching against human sacrifice; but we see from it that the patriarchs erected altars of heaped-up stone at which they did sacrifice.

Early ways of worship

The patriarchs had no priests; they conducted their own worship, and we do not know of any special ritual or of any particular times of worship. Here and there they set up pillars of stone, or *steles*, called *matzevot.* Jacob set one up near Shechem and named it *El-Elohe-Israel,* "God, the God of Israel" (Gen. 33:20). He set up another at Bethel, called *Bet-El,* "the House of God," a name used on many of our Temples today. Near Beer-sheba, Abraham planted a tamarisk tree, and he called the place *Adonai El Olam,* "My God, God of the World" (Gen. 21:33). The Bible often speaks of "high places" as places of worship, and this indeed follows a natural human impulse. From the stone altar on the high place comes the idea of a shrine, and then a temple.

Judaism in *outward* form in the time of the patriarchs may have been little different from the tribal religions around it. But it differed in its monotheism, repudiation of child sacrifice, and in the concept of the covenant. And it was to become still more different through its growth of ideas.

Originally there may have been seasonal festivals. Holidays such as Passover and Sukkot hark back to agricultural festivals which took place during the seasons of planting and harvest, as well as to lamb-birthing, times for the shepherds. These celebrations reach back to the days of the patriarchs.

Higher ways of thought

A casual view of Abraham's religion might claim that he felt no greater demand on himself and his people than to recognize the Oneness of God, and to maintain the covenant, marking it by circumcision. In addition, he observed tribal customs. About five hundred years later, we see that Moses brought down more rules connected to the covenant, by which the people took on themselves the Commandments and a whole set of laws, some of them enforcing the ancient tribal rules.

This does not mean that Abraham had no ethical conception of godly conduct. Many incidents in the Bible show us that Abraham was guided by a powerful sense of what is

Incense burned on this horned stone altar at Megiddo when David reigned.

right, so powerful indeed that he could even dispute with God about it.

In his dealings with men, the first patriarch is scrupulously fair, and a lover of peace. This is shown in the story of the well at Beer-sheba. To this day in the dry region of Beer-sheba, where Abraham settled, the Bedouin, whose tents and flocks remind us so much of the pastoral life in Biblical times, regard the tribal possession of a well as untouchable. It is an unwritten law in Bedouin life that they may kill a poacher using their well water. We may imagine that such customs go back all the way to Abraham's time, and we may read in the Bible how mindful he was to dig his own wells. Why was an incident of this kind repeated and handed down and finally written into the Bible? To show, of course, that Abraham was a righteous man.

Visitors to Beer-sheba today will have pointed out to them what are still said to be Abraham's wells. His was a true patriarchal personality. We know of his warmth, his consideration for others, his hospitality—as in the story of the generous welcome he gave to the strangers who, the Bible tells us, then proved to be angels, come to announce to the aging Sarah that she would yet give birth to a child.

The God relationship

The near-sacrifice of this same child, Isaac, provides us with our most profound and puzzling story of Abraham's God-relationship. It may be read simply as a lesson-for-the-neighbors—and for the clan itself—against human sacrifice, but it is also a story of man's readiness to accept the will of God, even to the most tragic degree. Yet this must be taken together with another story of Abraham's God-relationship, the story of his argument with God when the wicked city of Sodom was about to be destroyed. Will God spare the city for the sake of fifty good men? For ten? This is the other side of the sacrificial story of Isaac. If man must have complete faith in God, what of God's faith in man?

Though Lot is rescued, the city of Sodom is not spared. Abraham has faced the knowledge that one cannot bargain with creation. The whole way of worship that preceded Abraham, and that was to crop up again and again among the Jews and others after his time—was a way of bargaining with the gods, by flattery, or through sacrifice. Abraham saw that there was one God, unity in creation, and that while reverence was fitting and ennobling, God's laws of creation remained immutable.

For one man to have beheld a great truth does not mean that others will accept it from him. There is a legend which tells us that there came an old man, whom Abraham with his usual hospitality invited to his tent. But the old man would not join Abraham in his worship of the invisible, spiritual God, for he himself was a fire-worshiper, and he kept insisting that God was to be found only in the flames. Abraham could sometimes become angry, and this time he drove the heathen away. That night, the story continues, God appeared to Abraham in a vision and said, "I have borne with this ignorant man for seventy years; could you not patiently have suffered him for one night?"

The place of the patriarchs

Many of our prayers speak of the "God of Abraham, Isaac, and Jacob," almost as though this were a special deity. Originally, our sages differentiated them somewhat, speaking of *Magen Avraham*, Shield of Abraham, of *Paḥad Yitzḥak*, Fear of Isaac, and of *Avir Yaakov*, Master of Jacob. This too gives us an insight into the evolution of Judaism. Abraham, his son, and grandson are the three patriarchs whose lives span the first period of Judaism—the one in which it struggled to separate itself from surrounding idol-worship. The neighboring tribes, puzzled, might well have talked of the strange, invisible God of this clan. While Abraham is the true figure of the patriarch, his son Isaac, a gentle soul, did not change or develop the ways of his more active father. Then Jacob rounds out the period by the decisive act of burying his wife's household gods, his kinsman Laban's gods really, under a tree. Jacob was a roamer, more like his grandfather Abraham, and he too had a profound religious experience. Jacob's experience begins to shape Judaism as a religion of conscience.

It came to him quite a few years after he and his mother had deceived his aged and blind father about the birthright. They had wrapped the skin of a kid over Jacob's arm so that Isaac would mistake him for his hairier twin brother, Esau, the first-born. When Esau found out about this trick, the clever Jacob was so frightened that he fled from home. Years later, coming back with his wives and his flocks, he approached a meeting with Esau, and sleeping in a field, he had a mysterious dreamlike struggle with a "stranger," wrestling with him all night long. In the morning he found that a sinew of his thigh had been "touched" so that he limped. Jacob understood the stranger to have been an angel, and he called the place holy. Also, in accordance with the angel's instructions, he changed his name to Israel. And this name was to remain the name of our people.

From Abraham, a patriarch with a serene sense of right, we come to a portrait of a divided and troubled grandson, Jacob, faced with ethical problems in his daily life and personal relationships, and hoping to be able to do that which he felt God showed him was right. He too in his turn became the patriarch, but a patriarch who had suffered in his testing, the one who first gave us our insight into moral struggle.

So that the God of Abraham, Isaac, and Jacob is already growing in conception. He is the *El-elyon*, the all-inclusive God of Creation, reaching into the consciousness and the conscience of man.

4 Judaism in ancient Israel

Several centuries passed between the time of the wandering patriarchal tribes and the time when the Jewish people came back from slavery in Egypt to settle in villages and towns in their own land. During those years Judaism had changed. It had become a religion with a class of priests and very precise rituals of worship.

Moral and civil law

Another part of Judaism had been growing at the same time, a part that has much to do with the Judaism of today. That is the moral law.

During the centuries from Jacob-called-Israel to David, we know how the tribes went to Egypt, settled there, and were later enslaved. We know little or nothing about the religious practices of the Jews in Egypt. But we do know that when Moses led them out, he proclaimed an entire set of laws for them. The greatest and most profound of these laws, binding religious worship to moral conduct, were the Ten Commandments. The other laws of Moses that we find in the Torah, laws dealing with daily life, marriage, inheritance, diet, debt, and crime, were a complex mixture of religious, spiritual, civil, and tribal laws. Some probably were not too different from customs that had already been in practice. For example, stories about inheritance laws, going back to the time of the patriarchs—like the birthright story of Jacob and Esau—show us that there already were strictly followed rules in the clan.

It is not the complex code of law but the basic set of moral laws that is carried by Moses down to the people, inscribed on tablets of stone. Though the stone tablets are revered, this is not because of some magical powers, but because of the divinely inspired moral laws engraved on them.

Priests and rituals

Priests are installed, with Aaron, the brother of Moses, as High Priest, his sons as priests, and the other members of their tribe, the Levites, as helpers. From this alone we see that there were elaborate religious ceremonials; we read of processions, of chorals of harpists and singers.

Through forty years of desert life, this form of worship becomes fixed. The Ark is carried with them through the conquest of Canaan, and the twelve tribes separate to live in their different areas in the country. As they divide and spread out, the energy of each tribe centers on holding its ground. They mingle with the inhabitants, some tribes more readily than others. They intermarry, adapt or assimilate, as we now say,

Emblems of the twelve tribes of Judah are shown in this silver relief plaque (nineteenth century) from Palestine. Can you identify some of them from Jacob's blessing, Genesis 49?

and many begin to worship local idols. Yet there are members of the priestly family in the different areas, conducting ritual sacrifices, for we read later on how David called them together for a conclave at Hebron.

Times of the Judges

Meanwhile the authority over the communities, the settling of disputes, seems to have come into the hands of tribal "Judges." These were individuals like Gideon and Samson, Samuel, and the woman Deborah, each of whom rose up by strength of personality. According to tradition, the Judges, who sprang up in the different tribes, ruled the Israelites from the death of Joshua until the anointing of Saul as King of Israel. Some of the Judges, like Samuel, were also prophets. Deborah was both Judge and prophetess. But most of the Judges acted as military captains in times of war with the neighboring tribes, and as civil leaders and judges in peacetime.

The reign of Saul

The creation of the Kingdom came about through a Judge who was also a prophet. Samuel was an inspired person who spoke with the Voice of the Lord. He called the Hebrew tribes to unity. Widely, the argument arose that the people could be better protected from attack and from the influence of idol-worshiping neighbors only through a central authority. That meant a king. Samuel warned the farmers of all the evils that a

king might bring: he would tax them for his luxuries, he would take their sons for his army. But finally Samuel himself saw no other way than to choose them a king. There was a farmer named Saul who called the tribes to a unified battle against a coastal people, the Philistines, who kept encroaching up the hills. The prophet Samuel anointed Saul as King.

The troubled reign of Saul is devoted to wars and the building of the nation, and has little of spiritual quality. The Jews seem to have fallen back a few steps in the struggle between religion as a form of magic and religion as a form of conscience. There is so much dependence on soothsayers and those we would call *mediums*, who consult with ghosts, that Saul forbids people to deal with them, and even puts them out of the country. Then in later years he himself, on a famous occasion, consults the witches.

Meanwhile, Saul is considered by Samuel to be disobedient to the word of God in other ways. And so Samuel is inspired to seek out a new king. Among the sons of a Bethlehem farmer, named Jesse, the prophet feels led to choose the youngest, the gifted young poet and shepherd, David, who sings songs of prayer to the Lord. And Saul anoints David to be the future King.

It is when David follows Saul to the throne that the spiritual quality of Judaism again emerges. David's first act is to call together the priests and the Levites, who were scattered "in their cities and suburbs." They meet in Hebron, a city of deep traditional ties, for there the patriarchs lie buried in the cave purchased by Abraham. It is David's decision to "bring back the Ark of our God to us, for we sought not unto it in the days of Saul."

In other words, the great symbol of law, of conscience, has been half forgotten. Captured by the Philistines, it had brought them only bad luck, they said. They blamed it for epidemics in their cities and decided to hand it back to the Jews. It was left at a border town and then brought to the house of a man named Abinadab, in Kiriath-jearim. It stayed there until David decided to restore it as a central symbol of worship.

The tribes had fought together under Saul to form a nation, but they had not found inner unity. David, though a war hero, felt that such unity had to be spiritual. He had never wavered from the Jewish faith. Though he was a professional soldier who had once, when he fled from Saul, even sold his services to the Philistines, David was loyally religious. He envisioned a central Temple, which would not only do appropriate honor to the sacred tablets bearing the words of God, but would restore a true unity to the people through their faith.

David had captured the city of Jerusalem, and built himself a stronghold there. Now he put forward a simple question: How could a man build a house for himself, and not build a house for the Lord? But just as Moses had failed to enter the Promised Land, so David was not to build the Temple. He was to make all the preparations, but as a warrior, a man who had shed blood—and here we already see Judaism returning to the ways of conscience—it was not for David to erect the House of the Lord.

The return of the Ark

There are many fascinating tales in Jewish lore about the bringing back of the Ark to Jerusalem, where it remained in a tent, awaiting the building of the Temple. Some of the legends have a magic quality, and some have a moral quality.

The Bible tells how the Ark was moved in a cart, and when the oxen stumbled over a threshing floor, a man named Uzza put out his hand to steady the Ark. Instantly he was smitten and died—perhaps, we would conjecture today, in shock at his own awesome act in touching the holy Ark.

David is said to have been so shaken by this that he left the untouchable Ark in that same place for several months. Only when he heard that the people of that house were richly blessed during those months, did David feel free to return and take the Ark to Jerusalem.

Another wondrous tale, with a moral, is found among the Talmudic legends that enlarge on events described in the Bible. This one tells how on the last stages of the journey the priests took hold of the Ark to lift it from the oxcart, and were thrown violently to the ground. King David turned to a man of wisdom, Ahithophel, who smiled knowingly but offered no explanation or advice. Ahithophel, it seemed, just then felt peevish because the King had raised other wise men to court favor, over his head.

King David uttered a curse "on him who knows a remedy but withholds it from the sufferer." Only at this did Ahithophel explain that the priests had been cast down because God was offended that they consigned the Ark to an oxcart instead of carrying it aloft on their shoulders.

The idea that the holding back of helpful knowledge is a sin, which is what King David implied in his curse, is already a refined idea in ethics, and had been cited in the laws of Moses. It recognizes the guilt in what are called "sins of omission"—the failure to do what it would be naturally right and helpful to do. The holding back of needed knowledge is like holding back food and water from a hungry or thirsty man—even if he is your enemy. It is like holding back protection and provision for the widow or orphan.

The sin of omission is in some ways like the "indirect crime" such as we find exposed in the case of King David himself, years later when he came to be accused by the prophet Nathan of the murder of one of his captains, Uriah the Hittite (II Sam. 12).

It was, as we know, Nathan the Prophet, who came before the King to accuse him of this murder—a vivid example of a man of God accusing even a king. It is also an example of responsibility for crime, even when it consists of giving an order rather than committing the act itself. And a third point in Judaism is revealed in this moving incident; why was it Nathan the Prophet, rather than the High Priest of that day, who made the accusation? Even at this early period, we see two sides of Judaism, the priests are involved in ceremony and formal worship, while the prophets are concerned with jus-

This bas relief of the holy Ark was cut on a now-fallen pillar of the synagogue at Capernaum (Kefar Naḥum) built near Lake Kinneret in Roman times.

tice. And it is the prophets who are considered the men of God.

Religious ceremony in David's time still leaned to the side of magic, with sacrifices and auguries. For moral leadership, people turned to the inspired leaders called prophets. We may trace something of this same division in religious leadership down to our own times. There are many rabbis who, in addition to ritual observance, put much energy into social and moral problems, so that we hear it said that they are like the prophets of old.

Formal worship in David's time

As to formal religion in David's day, we are told, in Chronicles, exactly how this was organized in the tent or the large tabernacle where the Ark was then kept. David had called together the descendants of Aaron the High Priest. We have a list, with the precise order of their ranks, in the Bible. The priests drew lots for the most important positions, such as who should be governor of the sanctuary, and even for the sequence in which they should enter the tabernacle.

After the priests' positions were determined, the Levites were gathered.

Their office was to wait on the sons of Aaron for the services of the house of the Lord, in the courts, and in the chambers, and in the purifying of all holy things, and the work of the service of the house of God;

Both for the showbread, and for the fine flour for the meal offering, and for the unleavened cakes, and for that which is baked in the pan, and for that which is fried, and for all manner and sizes,

And to stand every morning to thank and praise the Lord, and likewise at even;

And to offer all burnt sacrifices unto the Lord in the Sabbaths, in the new moons, and on the set feasts, by number, according to the order commanded unto them, continually before the Lord. . . .   —I Chronicles 23:28–31

This is a complicated system of worship, and it seems no wonder that the priests for such a ritual did not occupy themselves overmuch with ethical problems of daily life. So the prophets arose.

Authority of the prophets

Who were the prophets, really? There was Samuel (both Judge and prophet), who could choose a king, and Nathan who could accuse a king. We know of no personalities such as these in other religions of the time.

A prophet was a person who was "called," a term we use even today. We are told that Samuel, when serving as a child at the shrine of Shiloh, heard himself called three times in one night; at first he thought it was the High Priest Eli calling his name, until Eli told him no, and that if he heard the voice again it was surely the voice of the Lord.

So, the prophets rose from among the people; they did not have to be members of the priestly clan. Judaism still depended on revelation through a personality, like Abraham, like Moses, even when it had become a tightly organized religion.

If the people heard a man's words again and again, and what he told them seemed inspired and right, he rose to esteem and acquired the authority of a prophet. His authority was not always enough to protect him from the rulers, for we know of prophets who were cast into dungeons. And there must have been many prophets who simply vanished from history, not much listened to, their words unrecorded. Yet through these inspired men, Judaism continued as a religion of conscience even while it became a formal institution.

The nation itself, as it took form under King David, felt that it was receiving God's continuing blessing, or what was called *hesed,* the divine concern that had been promised for the descendants of Abraham if they would keep the covenant.

The late Dr. Yehezkel Kaufmann pointed out that David, and notably his son Solomon, were successors to the Judges. Like Samson, these kings carried on military and civil tasks, while they had no "cultic" role. David is neither a Temple official, nor a prophet, though many of our psalms are said to have been written and sung by him. He is simply a worshiper. He speaks to God from his own heart and the heart of his people, but he does not perform miracles or wonders, nor does he speak for God, as prophets do when they declare "Thus said the Lord."

Great symbols of Judaism

David's kingdom is the beginning of a new period. Israel will be rooted to the land, and Jerusalem will be her capital. David himself became a religious symbol. His personal effect on the Jewish psyche was so great, and remained so great after his death, that when the Jews dreamed of salvation they dreamed of a David image. They did not cry out for Messiah, Son of Abraham, or Son of Moses, but for Messiah, Son of David.

The central religious symbol in David's time, as in the time of Moses, is again the Ark. "The Ark, hitherto a portable sacrum, housed in a tent, was unconnected with any particular place," Professor Kaufmann reminds us. It was David's idea to centralize all worship in Jerusalem. Thus, the Temple that would be built to house the Ark was to become the eternal symbol of the Israelite religion, a symbol that could not be erased even by physical destruction. Twice the Temple was to be torn down; except for a small section of one wall, the Temple has not existed physically for nineteen hundred years. It is still the Temple dreamed of by David and first built by his son Solomon.

Morality and ceremony

And yet because the Ark existed as "a portable sacrum" before the Temple, the idea of portability was already there when the first exile came. The idea that the Torah is present wherever Jews may wander exists in Judaism together with the idea that the Torah is enshrined in Jerusalem no matter how many times the Temple is torn down. This double image enabled the Jews to keep their faith when they were taken into exile.

They remembered, too, how David, an inspired singer of prayers to the Lord, was not acceptable to build His Temple because of his participation in bloodshed. Thus, from the time of David, the moral law of the prophets, and the ritual law of the priests, put their imprint on Judaism. The powerful stream of conscience voiced by the prophets, alongside the priestly ceremony of worship, gave Judaism its particular character. We might say that everything afterward was a refinement of these two strains. David's tabernacle became Solomon's Temple. After the destruction of the Temple, the rituals of priestly sacrifice were suspended, but certain other forms of worship developed, rites, and repetitions of prayer-texts that were like the chantings of the Levites in the Temple. When Passover could no longer be celebrated in the courtyard of the Temple, the Jews chanted, in their Seder at home, the very same psalms that the Levites had chanted in the Temple court-yard. And these same psalms still form part of our prayers today.

Through the centuries, the more pagan aspects of these sacrificial rites dwindled away; there were no more altars for the ceremony, since no other place could be substituted for the Temple in Jerusalem. But other forms of service and ceremony developed in our synagogues. A vestige of the priesthood remained, in our special rules that apply to the Cohens, and descendants of Cohens. On the moral side, of course, the Law needed no Temple, it could be practiced everywhere, and so our Biblical rules of conduct have been ceaselessly debated, and adapted, and refined, by Scribes, by Rabbis, by Talmudists, down to our very day.

Prophets of reform

It is fascinating that after Deborah and Samuel, the nation-building prophets, the era of the inspirational and reformist prophets coincided with the era of the First Temple, and of the Davidic line. It is as if in some mystical way all three are linked together.

The voices of this second group of prophets were heard at intervals through nearly four centuries, beginning with King David and ending with the return from Babylonian exile. During the tense and tragic decades preceding the fall of the kingdom, and during the half-century of exile, the most exalted of our poet-prophets produced illuminations that have ever since given light to the world.

And after these prophets, there did not again appear men who spoke with the voice of God, declaring Thus says the Lord. It was —as some modern philosophers describe it— as though God had taken pause, as though having already revealed to man the ethos of creation, God waited for man to show his understanding. In the same way a teacher may wait for signs that the first stages of a problem are understood, before going deeper into the subject.

During these centuries of rule by David's descendants, with good kings and bad, with royal alliance-marriages sometimes bringing a return to idol-worship, it often seemed as though all that Moses had taught was lost.

A power-group grew from among the wealthy landowners and the royal and priestly families; oppression and poverty increased. Yet again and again prophets arose to call the people back from superstition and the rulers from iniquity.

Sometimes, as Hannah Grad Goodman has written in *The Story of Prophecy*, the prophets were themselves sons of the establishment, like many reformers and revolutionists in our own time. Thus, Isaiah of Jerusalem, and Jeremiah, and Zechariah, were themselves from priestly families. Other prophets, such as Amos and Elijah, were herdsmen. And while they could, like Jeremiah, deal with immediate political issues, they constantly called out with the Voice of the Lord on questions of morality and conscience.

We can see a broadening of social concern, a more insistent universalism, and a more profound grasp of the intent of history, in the course of prophetic revelation. It becomes the counterpoint to Temple worship; it is the continuation of Torah. Again and again we are told that it is not the aroma of the burnt offering, but the deed of justice, that God loves.

Two stories show the growth of social consciousness. In both, a prophet confronts a king. In the first, Nathan accuses David of a brutal moral crime in having taken the wife of one of his captains, while sending the captain into mortal danger. In the second, it is Elijah, who accuses Ahab of having caused a farmer to be executed on trumped-up charges because he coveted the man's vineyard.

Micah howled against the treatment of the poor, against those who "rob the skin off them, and their flesh off their bones," against a Jerusalem where "leaders judge for bribes" and priests "teach for a price."

And Amos universalized the concern of God, reminding the Israelites, "Are you not as the children of the Ethiopians to Me? . . ." For even as He had brought Israel out of Egypt, He had rescued "the Philistines from Caphtor, and Aram from Kir."

Elijah, returning to Sinai to meditate on the Mount of Moses itself, brought the concept of individual responsibility, the "still small voice" of conscience. And in a further step, Ezekiel reversed the doomlike maxim that the sins of the fathers are visited on the sons, when he declared that each individual soul is from God, and therefore that each man is responsible and punishable for his own actions alone.

Above all came the concept of a divine goal, of all history as the working-out of Creation, in which Man takes part, toward a messianic fulfillment in which man shall "study war no more."

These wondrous illuminations come to us from prophetic Judaism, that flourished in the time of the Temple, that became part of our prayer services, and whose voice has not been heard since. But perhaps that is because, in these revelations, there has been enough for us to work toward for nearly twenty-five hundred years.

5 Judaism without ritual sacrifice

We have seen that Judaism, in its beginnings, was a patriarchal religion, breaking away from surrounding religions by belief in a single God, and by rejection of human sacrifice. Even when the Jewish tribes became a people, their leader was still a patriarchal figure, Moses. And Moses became the great lawgiver who interpreted the will of God, down to detailed rules about the treatment of slaves, among a people who had just emerged from slavery. When the people grew in numbers and scattered over a larger area, they were held together by these religious ordinances, some of which we would today consider in the area of civil law.

For common defense, and for religious unity and solidarity, the tribes united into a kingdom. Their first two kings were chosen by a religious leader, Samuel, and for the next thousand years Judaic ideas of government continued to be theocratic. Actually the tribes were not long able to maintain a united and independent kingdom. The northern tribes, breaking away from Judah after the death of Solomon, set up their capital in Samaria. Weakened by repeated dynastic overturns—and perhaps by their toleration of pagan rites and influence—they were defeated by the Assyrians (721 B.C.E.), their capital sacked and their people dispersed.

In Judah, to the south, the tribes of Benjamin, Levi, and Judah remained bound together by loyalty to the House of David, and by Temple worship. Both palace and Temple were in Jerusalem. The fabric of Jewish life was unified.

When the remaining tribes finally lost the southern kingdom (70 C.E.), both palace and Temple proved to be only the outward garments of Judaism, which showed itself able to survive without them. The conscience of the Jew, the spirit that wants to make divine law live in human relationships, worked on, even in the absence of kings and priests.

The divine spokesman, the prophet, kept appearing. He had had his place among them even before the palace and the Temple were destroyed. When the nation was under attack he was there in the person of Jeremiah, to tell them that godliness was even more vital than nationhood. And they also heard Micah telling them that God doesn't need them to burn sheep to Him on their altars, but only wants them to do what is right.

Assurbanipal, last of the great Assyrian emperors, is shown in this relief as a cavalry officer. Assyrian warriors were known for their cruelty and their ill-treatment of prisoners. Their capital was Nineveh. (See Jonah 4.)

Exile and return

Both kings and high priests prove to be less important than the voice of conscience in this developing idea called Judaism. When the kingdom of Judah is first destroyed by the Babylonian invader, and the Temple is in ruins, it is the search for a right way to live, it is this growing and developing set of laws-around-religion, that keeps the Jews from disappearing as other conquered peoples do.

They come back to Jerusalem from their first exile in Babylon, with these laws; they build the Temple anew, they revive their system of Temple worship, even though under foreign rule. For only some fifty years have passed and they have not yet fallen away from the idea of altars and sacrificial rites. Yet they pay growing attention now to the open reading of their laws, which they had held to in Babylon, even while they had no Temple sacrifices.

A short-lived theocracy

Finally, when their foreign rulers change from Babylonians to Syrians, and the new ones try to interfere with the practice of their religion, they revolt. A priestly family leads the revolt against the occupying Syrians, and once more the Jews become a self-ruling nation in their own land. This time royalty and priesthood are one and the same: the Maccabees.

Neither David nor Solomon had attempted such rule. The control of both synagogue and state by one family leads to an aristocratic theocracy, a rich and powerful upper class. And in a family struggle for the throne, one side calls in a new Mediterranean power for help—the Romans. They stay. By 63 B.C.E. they take over. Their rulers are harsh; they extort heavy taxes for "protection." Some of the Jewish aristocrats become collaborators. However, the people as a whole fall back into their character as a religious group.

Scholars, scribes, and rabbis

The democratic spirit, expressed in the voice of the prophets, has not died. It is now expressed in quieter voices, in the voices of scholars and scribes. They do not cry in the wilderness; they teach in schools and in study halls that are part of the synagogues. They are seekers of wisdom, like Hillel. They do not say that they speak with the voice of the Lord; they speak with the voice of the Law.

From the time of the exile in Babylon, the role of the teacher, or rabbi, had been growing. Exile raised many problems of Jewish community life, debated by the rabbis, who tried to fit the rules of life in the Holy Land to life in Babylon. And after the return to Jerusalem, the rabbis continued in their role. Life under the occupying power raised more problems. To solve them, a *Sanhedrin*, a congress of rabbis and priests, was established.

When the Maccabean interlude of self-rule was ended, and the new occupying power, the Romans, finally destroyed the Second Temple (70 C.E.), and with it every vestige of a Jewish kingdom, there remained the teachers, the rabbis. This time the age of the sacrificial altar was definitely ended. The ancient ritual adornment of Judaism was gone. The faith had to live on its content alone.

The messianic hope

Part of that content is the Jewish belief that the world is perfecting itself, that a time of goodness will come when nations will learn war no more, when peace and plenty and brotherhood will prevail. And this hope had been given expression in a word, an image—the Messiah. When Messiah comes, people will be good to each other, God's way will be accepted on earth.

But aside from the visionary dreams of a Messiah and of messianic times, this idea of a world that somehow learns goodness had been growing among the Jews for several centuries, growing as their troubles grew. As the Jews fell under one conqueror after another, as they went through the Babylonian exile, and the return, and new invasions, and underground struggles, and revolt, and crucifixions at the hands of the Romans, the longing for the Messiah kept growing.

Jesus of Nazareth

Such a longing for a leader, in other lands, among other people, has given rise to military heroes, and to dictators as well. One can never be certain to what this freedom-longing leads. Among the Jews, during the hard rule of the Romans, two men were to be mistakenly proclaimed as Messiah. They appeared in the times of great Rabbis, from Hillel to Akiva. The first was a folk preacher and healer in the Galilee, called Yehoshua ben Yosef, known to us as Jesus of Nazareth.

He was a reformer, a friend of the poor, an opponent of the privileged, a prophetic personality. According to the stories that have come down to us in the New Testament, he came with his followers to Jerusalem for Passover and made a stormy scene in the Temple, chasing out the money-changers. He did not want to change the Jewish laws of observance, he declared, but he was against corruption.

When he let it be suggested that he was the Messiah, the Temple priests were upset, as this was blasphemy, and then the Romans condemned the preacher as a rebel, and crucified him. Later his followers declared he was the Messiah, Son of God. The worship of a man on earth as a deity was of course against the spiritual conception of Judaism, and so this group eventually created a religion among the gentiles, built on the messianic idea. So, just as the thousand years of Temple rituals and sacrifices, interrupted only by the fifty years in Babylon, was coming to an end with the last destruction of the Temple, the moral idea of messianic times became stronger in Judaism, and even spread to the gentile world.

After the failure of Jesus as a Messiah, the last throes of the struggle in Jerusalem took place, with underground resistance, mass crucifixions, defeats, revolts, a four-year war, and crushing defeat again.

The life of Rabbi Akiva

What happens in such a time? People suffer, but live. There are still rich and poor. One Jew whose name we revere lived through the entire period, to the age of ninety-two, only then to be executed by the Romans. His name was Akiva, and he became connected with another mistaken Messiah, Bar Kokhba.

That Akiva was poor as a boy, that he married a remarkable woman, that he began to study only with his own son, and other such tales of his life, we have read. But his long lifetime shows us what was happening to Judaism under stress.

Akiva was born about fifteen years after Yehoshua ben Yosef made a famous rabbinical-sounding response to the Romans: "Render unto Caesar what is Caesar's, and unto God what is God's." It was a way of saying that he, as a Jew, did not oppose Roman tax collections. But it was also a way of saying that the occupying power should keep its hands off religion. Today we would call this separation of church and state.

By the time Akiva was grown up, the Roman Caesars were trying to take what was God's. They even decided to seize the Temple treasury, and at this point the resistance movement broke into open revolt, a revolt that ended after siege, starvation, heroism, and carnage, in the fall of Jerusalem. For the second time the Temple was destroyed.

The shepherd Akiva was one of the young men who felt that the Jewish community would nevertheless survive, by its own inner laws. After the fall of Jerusalem, when Judaism was preserved by Rabbi Yohanan ben Zakkai's setting up an academy at Yavneh, Akiva came there to study.

The first director of the college was a still-wealthy landowner, Eliezer ben Hyrkanos, who was described as "a plaster-lined cistern from which not a single drop can leak out." Poor students were not welcomed by this man, who believed that a scholar should be free of financial worries. So Akiva went to Joshua ben Hananya, a former singer in the Temple, who, since there was no more Temple, had become a needlemaker.

Akiva was admitted to the needlemaker's Torah school, but his teacher, Tarfon, found his social views too radical. Akiva changed colleges. Having already gained renown as a bright scholar, he was now accepted into the wealthy man's school, and after fifteen years he departed to found his own academy, in B'nei B'rak, where he commonly lectured under a favorite fig tree.

Akiva's teachings

What did he lecture about? In Temple times, the Rabbis had concerned themselves with all sorts of ceremonial questions, such as whether a knife for the sacrifice may be sharpened on the Sabbath. Now, Akiva turned more and more toward the social side of the Law, as may be seen in the analysis of a modern scholar, Rabbi Louis Finkelstein of the Jewish Theological Seminary. He summarizes Akiva's teachings as follows:

1. Whatever the inequalities in the world, we must not let them intrude in the worship of God. Thus, no ceremonies should be used in which the poor cannot partake without heavy sacrifices. (One thinks of expensive Bar Mitzvahs in our own time.)

2. When civil law is not rigidly fixed, but still open to interpretation, it should be interpreted so as to correct social inequalities. It should be used to favor the slave, women and children, the artisan, the plebeian.

3. Women's rights should be extended. (With this, Akiva aroused violent opposition.

It was then the custom for a married woman who worked to turn over all her earnings to her husband. Akiva ruled that if she earned more than her keep, the difference was her own. Akiva's own wife had devotedly helped him. When sages debated their favorite question, "What is true wealth?" one said, "To have a hundred vineyards and a hundred slaves to work them." Another said, "Contentment and satisfaction with what one has." Akiva said, "A wife who is comely in her deeds.")

4. The pious must be protected from handicaps that may result from their observance of religious law. (Today in Israel, since the observant storekeepers close their shops on Sabbath, so must their non-observant competitors.)

5. There is no room for superstition in Judaism. Tales of miraculous cures that various sects—such as the Christians—related were not to be believed as supernatural. Jews who resorted to magical cures were deemed unfit for immortal life.

6. The ideals of human equality were basic in religion. For example, if a rich, important man was injured in an accident, he should receive no more than a poor man for the same injury.

The Oral Law

As he gained prominence, Akiva was sent on a mission to a new emperor in Rome who, it was promised, would rebuild the Temple in Jerusalem. But Akiva came back more strongly convinced than ever that the Jews, Temple or no Temple, must hold firmly to their inner community life if they were to survive. It was then that he began his great work of bringing order into the mass of Oral Law, so as to make God's justice available wherever Jews lived.

One of his pupils said, "Akiva is like a merchant who goes about from farm to farm. Here he buys wheat, there he selects barley, and at another place, beans. When he comes home he sorts out the produce in respective bins. Thus Akiva goes from scholar to scholar, gathering our rulings, and then he proceeds to sort them out." It was a rather earthy comparison for a religious matter— and that in itself is Judaism.

The division of the Mishnah into six basic headings is said to go back to Akiva. His collection became the core of the collection of Rabbi Meir, which in turn served for the final version of Judah ha-Nasi, on which both the Babylonian and Jerusalem Talmuds, in use today, are based.

During many years, Akiva counseled pacifism, even though the Romans were ever more demanding. When they imposed the notorious *fiscus Judaicus,* a special tax on Jews not only in their land but all over the empire, Akiva said, "Pay it." When they promised to rebuild the Temple he advised the Jews not to despair should the promise be broken —as it was. Even during the first restrictions on worship, he reminded the Jews that what one Roman emperor decreed the next might cancel. But the decrees of Hadrian (118– 138 C.E.) took a drastic turn. Circumcision was forbidden. Next, observance of the Sabbath. Thus, Judaism was to die. Finally, the death penalty was decreed for ordaining a rabbi, and the punishment was carried out when Judah ben Baba was caught giving ordination to five of his pupils. Akiva at last showed his own form of resistance by defiantly continuing to teach, in the open, under his fig tree.

The Bar Kokhba revolt

At this time Bar Kokhba began his revolt, and Akiva, at ninety, supported the patriot who had aroused the messianic hope anew. Even though Bar Kokhba was not a very pious man, even though—according to historian Joseph Klausner—he was not of the House of David, Akiva, overcome with emotion when he saw Bar Kokhba's men conquering the "unconquerable" Roman legions, joined all Jewry in the cry of "Messiah! The Redeemer!" The aged rabbi went so far as to add a prayer in the Passover Seder saying, "Blessed art Thou, O Lord, who has redeemed Israel."

Then Akiva declared that the prophecy had been fulfilled that said, "There shall come forth a star out of Jacob," and plainly announced, "This is the messianic king."

With the adherence of Akiva, the total population swept behind Bar Kokhba, and actually drove the Romans from the land. For two years the Jews were free again, but no start was made on rebuilding the Temple, for Bar Kokhba used all his available resources in preparing for the return of the Romans in greater force than ever. They came, bringing their most famous legion, the tenth, all the way from Britain. The Emperor Hadrian himself crossed the sea. In the bloodiest of wars,

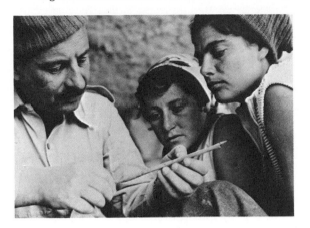

During the Bar Kokhba rebellion bands of Jews revolted against Rome. They were put down by Roman arrows such as the one Professor Yigael Yadin and his students are examining.

it took the Romans over three years to re-
conquer the Jews. Bar Kokhba fell in the
final slaughter at Betar (135 C.E.). Meanwhile Rabbi Akiva had been arrested, and
flayed to death in public, for teaching Jewish
Law.

The Talmudic era

Judea was devastated. But life somehow
went on in Galilee. A new Sanhedrin was
chosen, a call was issued for anyone who had
studied to come and teach, and anyone who
had not studied to come and learn. Akiva's
work on the Talmud was continued, and
though Jerusalem had been wiped from the
face of the earth, the Rabbis carried on with
the compilation that was in a few centuries
to become the Jerusalem Talmud.

The Talmudic era had begun. At another
period long before, Judaism had survived
without the Temple. But the sages knew that
it could not survive without Jewish Law.

One result of the total destruction of Jerusalem was the return of the use of Hebrew in
the academies and synagogues, as a memory
of Temple services. In the same way, centuries later in Europe when Yiddish was the
everyday language of Jewry, Hebrew was
required for study and prayer. It was known
as *Lashon ha-Kodesh*, the holy tongue.

*From this reconstruction we can see how
the synagogue at Capernaum looked when it
was built in the second or third centuries* C.E.
*Then, when the Jews of Galilee lived
under Roman rule, it served as a center
of learning and worship.*

Dispersal of the Jews

Though Jewish life in Galilee went on, a great
part of the rest of the country was empty, or

being refilled with foreigners. Masses of Jewish prisoners were sold abroad as slaves, and thousands and thousands of refugees had fled in all directions. This was the great dispersion. The already existing colonies of Jews in various Mediterranean cities were enlarged, while stray groups went further and further into Europe, Africa, and Asia in their search for a livelihood.

Jews spoke Greek in Greece and Egypt, Latin in Rome, Aramaic in Mesopotamia, but everywhere prayed in Hebrew. In the eyes of the world, these communities, from Babylon to Rome, were the same people. And despite the difficulty of travel and communication in those times, it is quite astonishing, according to Professor Gerson Cohen, to find a close similarity of customs in these scattered Jewish groups, no matter how different their surroundings. The prayers were now more uniform, though a Jew could add prayers of his own. A Passover in Crete was like a Passover in Alexandria. Professor Salo Baron tells us, "Perceiving how much its inner divisions had contributed to its downfall, the Jewish people now concentrated on achieving internal unity under single-minded rabbinic leadership."

A changing concept

Originally, from the lands of idol-worshipers, Jews had carried their faith in one God to their own land. Now dispersed from that land, they brought their faith in one God to various lands of pagan worship.

They also carried with them their hope of Messiah. We have seen that twice, under the Romans, the naming of a Messiah had raised enormous consequences. Strangely enough the scattering Jews found that the story of the first of these, Jesus, was spreading everywhere, and in a turned-about way. It was being used against the Jews, instead of against the Romans who had killed him. But the idea of messianic redemption remained with them; again and again, for centuries, Jews would overturn their lives, to follow a new *Mashiah*.

This messianic idea was eventually to change, to move away from the idea of a person to an idea of inner human redemption, just as the idea of God changed in Judaism from a personalized to a wholly spiritual conception.

A fence around the law

The messianic idea had been adopted by the gentiles through Christianity, indeed the entire Torah had been annexed in their religion, but they were mixing it up with what seemed to the Jews to be another kind of idol worship in which Ychoshua, or Jesus, was God. The Jews drew more firmly together to keep their beliefs free from such errors. The end of altar worship in a way had purified their religion, for it left them only the Torah. Now the Rabbis were determined to "put a fence around the Torah," a fence of other regulations and interpretations, that would prevent Jews from straying out to adopt the practices of people around them, to turn to a new form of idol worship. The fence held.

6 Religion faces logic

At the beginning of this book we took the point of view that a people grows the way a person grows, from the child's superstition and wonder, to the beginning of understanding, to reason. In the study of biology this process has been put into three high-sounding words: ontogeny recapitulates phylogeny; each single being repeats the stages of all beings.

What we have done here is to turn this rule around and look back over our religious growth as a group. We have watched the Jews going through the same stages of religious belief that a single person goes through, from childhood magic to a mature, reasonable faith. We saw Judaism growing out of primitive idol worship to the worship of one God, but still holding to a powerful system of taboos, and a sacrificial altar. We saw the growth of an ethos and the end of altar worship. But even when the altar is gone, taboos remain. The Talmud has refined, adapted, balanced, explained, interpreted this system, and kept it at one and the same time sacred, and yet adjustable to the variations of life. Let us now take a leap forward of a thousand years to a time of Jewish life, like the time of a person's maturing, when one seeks logical explanations that help us understand what we have already been taught as belief.

Jewish life in the twelfth century

The time of the great philosopher Maimonides—the twelfth century—is such a time. Only a very small part of the Jewish people, about forty thousand, were then living in Palestine, which had passed through several more ruling hands after the Romans. Tribes from the Arabian desert, followers of a religion newer than Christianity, had swept across the Holy Land, on their path of conquest. They were the Muslims. A few centuries later, the Christian Crusaders had come from France and England to take Jerusalem from the Muslims. They in turn were driven out by a later Muslim group, the Saracens. And all through this, the children of Abraham clung to a few centers, such as the ports of Acre and Gaza, keeping touch with Jewish communities in the outside world, now far more numerous than their own.

There was no Temple in Jerusalem, no central religious authority from which Jewish laws flowed, although churches and mosques abounded in the rebuilt city. Each Jewish community in the outside world, if it could not find its problems solved in the Talmud, wrote to some renowned scholar, perhaps Rashi in France, or Maimonides in Spain, for advice. Even the Jews of Palestine turned for answers to the learned community in Egypt, or to important Jewish colonies in North Africa, such as Fez in Morocco.

Traffic still flows in and out of the Damascus Gate of the old walled city of Jerusalem. Mosques and the domes of churches mark its skyline.

Muslims and Christians

Jews lived under Muslim rule in the Middle East, and under Christian rule in Europe. No longer were they the only people who saw unity in God. Virtually the whole civilized world had reached this stage of understanding, though with strong vestiges of idolatry.

The two religions that had grown powerful during this thousand years—and whose followers fought each other—had both been inspired by Judaism. The Christians, instead of being friendly to the Jews who had taught them the unity of God, despised them, persecuted them, and periodically massacred them. But they also engaged in serious theological disputes with them. Christians argued that their religion was the next step from, or in, Judaism, but the Jews saw it only as a step backward, since the Christ-figure had become a deity, and this was idolatry.

A somewhat similar pattern had taken place six centuries after Christianity was born. Again a preacher with a prophetic gift was inspired by early Judaism, though this time, unlike Jesus, he was not a Jew. In Mecca, where the Arabs, from ancient times, worshiped a black stone, there came a vision to a trader named Mohammed. He had contact with Jewish merchants, and from them learned a good deal about the Bible, for in his own holy book, the Koran, he was to repeat the stories of the patriarchs and various teachings, all in his own poetic way. Mohammed's visions and sayings, put together in the Koran, were to be spread by the sword. Fierce Arab horsemen set out to convert the world, crying, "There is only one God and Mohammed is His Prophet!" They built an empire from Spain to Turkey. And as though their collective mind had been jolted into activity by contact with the world, the Arabs had a high period of creativity in mathematics, science, medicine, poetry and philosophy.

The Greek philosophers

It was not the new religion but an older habit of philosophic thought that now challenged Judaism. Already, far back in the time of the Second Temple, when Alexander the Great had conquered Palestine, Judaism had had to face cool questioning minds in the Greek philosophers. Although the Greeks had brought their idols, they had also brought their logic. Their system of gods, their idol worship, was entirely scorned by pious Jews. But their system of thought was a challenge, particularly in such Greek cities as Alexandria, where there was a large Jewish community. And though through the centuries the Greek gods became mere story figures, the questioning logic of Socrates, the scientific, inquiring attitude of Aristotle, have remained to this day active agents in the thinking of most of mankind, including the Jews.

Let us take an example in Judaism of a challenge for which we have a typical Greek word—*anthropomorphism*. It means, as you know, thinking of God in human ways. Almost all religions have elements of anthropomorphism, and so does early Judaism. The

Bible is filled with examples. Did God speak in actual words to Moses? Did God have hands, to take clay and make Adam? Far back, it was already explained that these were symbols, ways of speech to help people understand a spiritual idea, but to this day there are many people who insist that they believe each word literally.

Another great challenge was the story of creation. As science began to develop in the time of Maimonides, intellectuals of his kind were faced by logical challenges. This pious Jew accepted the challenge. His correct name was Moses ben Maimon, and we already know the saying, "From Moses to Moses there was none like Moses." Though he was not so much a discoverer as a clarifier, in fame he might be called the Einstein of his time. And just as Einstein sought to discover a unified field theory and prove mathematically the perfect unity of creation, so, with the limited science of his time, Maimonides stressed the unity and perfection of creation to explain the unity of God. Thus he used logic to prove the very existence of God.

Social contacts of the Jews

We have a common notion about the Jews of those times being huddled in their ghettos, and having only business contacts with the outside world. But though religious life and family life were enclosed, the Jews circulated a good deal and were in social contact with the people of most of the lands where they lived. There was an interchange.

Rashi, for example, refers to works in the French language as *bil'shoneynu,* "in our tongue," and Jews used prayer books in French showing, even then, a high degree of acculturation. Jewish mothers used local French lullabies for their babies, and conversely Christian priests must have learned synagogue melodies, for such melodies found their way into the Catholic service.

In Germany, too, certain local customs were adapted into Jewish life. Some of them became so "Jewish" that their origin was forgotten. The braids in Sabbath bread are said to be an imitation of a German bread in which braids of dough replaced woven locks of hair sacrificed in fertility rites.

Another of our customs, *Tashlikh,* on the second day of Rosh Hashanah, when we throw crumbs from our pockets into a body of water, was in pagan times no doubt an offering to the water spirits. We explain it as a symbolic casting away of our sins.

Not only in France and Germany do we have signs of intermingling of cultures. The Jews of Spain, when Arabs ruled that country, generally wrote in Arabic, using Hebrew, as elsewhere, only for their religious works —though for poetry, too. And it was oddly enough through Arabic that Jewish scholars again came into contact with classic Greek thinking, for the culturally awakened Arabs were now themselves discovering this material. In the ninth century the Caliphs in Baghdad set up a center for the translation of Greek works on astronomy, medicine, and philosophy. Thus, we see a cosmopolitan atmosphere developing, with a mixture of cultures. How would Judaism fare in this light?

Inquiry and intellectual challenge

The intellectual circles of Baghdad, Rabbi Simon Noveck tells us, were made up of "agnostics, parsees, materialists, atheists, and Jews," as well as of Muslims. There was a lively atmosphere of inquiry. All beliefs were under challenge. The same cosmopolitan exchange of ideas took place in other Muslim centers such as Cairo and Cordova, and Cordova was the city where Maimonides grew up.

The challenge of the reasoning mind was extended to such beliefs as divine providence, immortality, freedom of will, to such questions as the existence of God, to the problem of good and evil. Judaism had to be justified for intellectual Jews who were wavering in their faith, even as today.

The historian Isaac Husik tells us:

The Bible and the Talmud were documents of revelation, Aristotle was the document of reason. . . . What was required was . . . to show that the conflicting passages in the Scriptures are capable of interpretation so as to harmonize with each other and with the results of rational speculation. . . . As long as the Jews were self-centered and did not come in close contact with an alien civilization of a philosophic mold, the need for a carefully thought out and consistent theory . . . was not felt.

The life of Maimonides

Now Rabbi Moses ben Maimon (also known by his initials as Rambam) felt this need.

Born in Cordova in 1135, he had studied the Talmud, then medicine, had moved with his family to Fez, then to Palestine, then to Fustat (Cairo) where he became physician to the Sultan. He died in 1204, and by his wish was buried in Palestine, where his tomb, in Tiberias, is a place of pilgrimage to this day.

We can get some idea of a busy Jewish doctor's life in those times from a letter written at the height of his career to his translator, Samuel ibn Tibbon.

. . . live at Fustat and the Sultan resides at Cairo; these two places are about one mile and a half distant. My duties to the Sultan are very exacting. I am obliged to visit him every day, early in the morning. If he or any of his children, or any members of the harem, are indisposed, I am compelled to spend the greater part of the day in the palace. Then too, it frequently happens that some of his couriers fall sick and I must tend to the healing. Hence as a rule I find it necessary to stay in Cairo till late in the afternoon. When I return to Fustat, I am almost dead with hunger. [For he observed kashrut.] On my arrival I find the waiting room of my home filled with people, both Jews and Gentiles, rich and poor, judges and bailiffs, friends and foes—a mixed multitude who wait to consult me about their illness . . . when the last patient has gone I am so exhausted I can scarcely speak.

The Mishneh Torah

And yet this man found time to compose answers to Jewish questions from far away. For example, there is his famous letter answering the Yemenites, who asked how to keep their people from believing in a false

The great religious code, the Mishneh Torah, has often been copied and printed since its completion in 1180. These pages are from a printing in Rome in 1480.

messiah who had appeared there. Maimonides somehow found time to absorb the whole of Talmudic knowledge and codify it in his Mishneh Torah. This work was even more amazing than the codification of Rabbi Akiva, since by the time of Maimonides there was so much more to consult. "All the interpretations, codes and responses which the Geonim have written have become unintelligible in our days," he declared—

therefore I, Moses, the son of Maimon, the Spaniard, have girded my loins and put trust in the Lord . . . I have studied all these works . . . and expounded them in precise language, so that the entire Oral Law may be accessible to everyone without any arguments or counterarguments . . . In short, my intention is that not many may have need to resort to any other book on any point of Jewish law.

For his new code, he used philosophic and scientific arguments that were unknown before. Who, before, had felt the need for explaining God, for proving His existence? God was worshiped from within the Jewish soul. But Maimonides lived in a time of questioning; he proceeded to show there was a First Cause. His book was fiercely attacked, widely praised, and it led him to write another and even more famous work, *The Guide for the Perplexed.* This contained basic answers to so many human problems that it was taken up not only by Jews but by non-Jews, and was the first Jewish book, after the Bible, to become part of world literature. As the scholar Jacob S. Minkin comments, "The world had but a distorted knowledge of the Talmud, and even the Bible was twisted and tortured for partisan propaganda." The voice of Maimonides about Jewish faith, his philosophic thinking about problems that troubled the minds of men of other faiths as well, won new respect for the Jews.

"I believe"

The faith of Maimonides is crystallized in his Thirteen Creeds, his "I Believe." A modern rabbi, Israel Goldstein, has offered us his own understanding of these basic affirmations. "I believe with a perfect faith that the Creator, blessed be His name, is the Author and Guide of everything that has been created, and that He alone has made, does make, and will make all things." Rabbi Goldstein says, "It is quite consistent with the twentieth century, as it was with the twelfth century, as it was at the very beginning when the Book of Genesis was formulated, to assert, 'In the beginning God created...' "

The creeds go on to express faith in unity —one God—in incorporeality—"the Creator, blessed be His Name, is not a body but is free from all accidents of matter . . . He has not any form whatsoever." When Maimonides says, "I believe that God rewards those that keep His Commandments and punishes those that transgress them," Rabbi Goldstein comments, "I join in that belief wholeheartedly but not in the sense that some people take it. If you believe that the doing of good brings its reward immediately in tangible terms, then your level of thinking is not as high as it should be . . . *Mitzvah* . . . brings its own satisfaction, and therefore its own reward. The reward of doing good is that

you are the kind of person capable of doing that act."

What of the Rambam's statement, "I believe in the coming of the Messiah, and though he tarry, I will wait daily for his coming?" Today's rabbi points out that the idea of a personal messiah has been sublimated into the idea of a messianic age, toward which we are progressing. And this is in the spirit of the reply of the Rambam to the Yemenites and their problem with a false messiah. For his help, the Yemenites include his name in their prayers even now.

Maimonides pursued the path of reason, of rationalization, of logic, in Judaism. But the early science of his time could not explain everything. Even today science is far from knowing the First Cause, the act of creation. When logic is blocked, some men turn to intuition. When we stand before the unanswerable questions: What is God, Why does evil exist, How much free will does man possess, there are three possible responses. We may say: We cannot ever know. Or, let us use reason and try to find the answers bit by bit. Or, there is a secret way that only the initiates may know.

The Kabbalists

While Maimonides took the second way, of reason, the "secret" way was explored by a mysterious book written about his time, also by a Spanish Jew. This was the *Zohar*, the "Book of Splendor," by Rabbi Moses de Leon, who died in 1305. Before him, but less influential, was the work of Rabbi Judah, in Germany, called *Sefer Ḥasidim*. The word *ḥasid* is popular today, but we connect it

This gold amulet containing a Kabbalistic text was hung over a child's cradle to protect him from evil.

with an entirely different background, the sect of the Baal Shem Tov, who lived in the eighteenth century in the Carpathians. This earlier mystic stream exemplified in the *Sefer Hasidim* goes far, far back in the history of Jewish thought, and is often spoken of as *Kabbalah*.

Kabbalists believe that besides the plain words of the Bible there is a secret, inner meaning. There are various Kabbalistic systems for discovering this meaning. Some use the number values of each Hebrew letter, adding up the letters of a word and dividing the total into new words. The famous Kabbalist, Abraham Abulafia, believed the entire Bible was one huge cipher. Miraculous stories are told about the powers of the Kabbalists. But essentially they were searching for answers to the great questions concerning good and evil—and the question of the coming of the Messiah.

The breadth of Judaism

Judaism, challenged by the outer world, by new religions, by the beginnings of scientific inquiry, by the probings of philosophy, proved broad enough to hold the rational believer to his faith as well as the mystical Kabbalist. For Judaism sought God through the entire spectrum of human perception. It attained a maturity of view while retaining its youthful vigor.

Central leadership was gone, the nation and the Temple were gone, sacrificial worship was gone, but strict community laws, taboos, and ethical laws remained. Only, above them, from the scientist to the Kabbalist, was spiritual belief.

7 Judaism in our day

Abraham knew of the unity of God. That was the compact seed of his belief. He could not know just how this idea would unfold.

But it is said that Moses knew. It is said that in the Torah given to Moses there were not only the commandments and laws of his own time, but all the laws that were to come. The whole Talmud was there.

This legend can be understood if we follow the analogy of the seed, for does not the human seed contain every trait of the grown person, down to the color of each hair? So every subsequent rule, the pious believed, was foreseen in the laws of Moses.

The right of choice

Yet Judaism includes the belief in free will. Man is not the slave of a totally fixed and determined world, but has a share in deciding what will happen, since he can and must choose between right and wrong. In this way, Judaism is also free from rules that become obsolete; it may choose its path. Just as the individual has a hand in shaping his own character, so the people may shape itself. The Jews are still doing this through Judaism.

Emancipation and enlightenment

Until two or three centuries ago (and in a throwback to that time, under Hitler), Jews in many ways kept apart from other groups largely because they were forced to keep apart. They were segregated in ghettos; at times they were even made to wear yellow patches, or other distinctive items, such as the "Judenhut"—the Jew's-hat.

Then in the eighteenth century came the challenge of liberty and equality. Even the laws of *kashrut* began to be widely disregarded. What would this do to Judaism?

Two words appear, the great slogans of the period: enlightenment and emancipation. Enlightenment had already begun with wider reading through printing, with the sudden spurt of experimental science and exploration, with the writings of brilliant men like Voltaire. Social bonds were broken. Experimental science poured a blazing light on man's world.

Emancipation is the great word for liberation, the word used by Lincoln in freeing the slaves. For the Jews, emancipation began when the spirit of democracy arose. The American Revolution and the French Revolution confirmed the idea of the equality of man, and from one country to another the Jew, not without strife, eventually became an equal citizen. Some lands granted equality in one step, and in others, as in Russia, equality came slowly—the last laws against the Jews were swept aside only with the Revolutions of 1917, and to our day, the Jews in the Soviet Union do not have equality

The community life of the Jews in Prague centered around the Jewish City Hall, shown here. The famous Altneuschul (not shown) is at the left.

with other groups in such essential matters as teaching their own culture.

As social revolutions began, many Jewish intellectuals saw these changes as taking the place, for them, of Judaism itself. Some assimilated, or tried to lose themselves in one "movement" or another. But for others, the new sense of equality made them more at ease in their Jewish identity.

To the ghetto Jews, forbidden by their religious leaders from reading "unholy" books, confined to the Talmud, enlightenment was in itself a kind of emancipation.

Results of the enlightenment

We all know the trick of propping an exciting adventure story behind an open geometry textbook. But for the *yeshivah baḥur* it was the exciting geometry textbook that was propped behind his open rabbinic tome. Our parents' grandfathers might still tell about this, for "enlightenment" did not conquer all at once; "outside" knowledge was bitterly opposed, and the struggle went on across several generations. Enlightenment shook up the life of the *shtetl* in Eastern Europe, it produced scientists like Chaim Weizmann, revolutionists like Leon Trotsky, and also great Jewish scholars like the historian Simon Dubnov.

It produced atheists and agnostics and socialists and Zionists. Many people thought it would be the end of Judaism. Instead, together with the movement of emancipation that had roots in Germany, it opened a great era in Jewish thinking and brought changes in forms of observance in Progressive, Reform, Liberal, and Conservative as well.

Most importantly, it brought an intense examination of what we believe in. The great eternal questions were examined afresh, perhaps only to be given the same answers in new words, perhaps only for us to say we cannot know the answers. Yet we must ask, what is Judaism now? Is it still different from other ways of religious thinking? How much of what we believe did Abraham believe? And vice versa? How much of what David believed, do we believe? Of what Maimonides believed? Is there still one Judaism?

The Jewish world today

We read that in the early centuries after the fall of the Temple, a Jew from Spain would find himself at home in a synagogue in Baghdad. Does a Jew from Morocco today find anything in common with the Reform Jew from Miami? Do they believe in the same God? In the same Torah? Does the Israeli *kibbutznik* or the student at the University in Jerusalem have much in common with either of them? And what do we ourselves want in Judaism?

We have made this brief, giant-step review of the development of Judaism so as to be able to set our own ideas in line with what has gone before. Now it will also be useful to look around us and see what we mean by the Jewish world today.

From a population of a few million in

their own land when conquered by the Romans, plus another few million in the Diaspora of that time, Jews at the beginning of this century numbered some sixteen million. They were spread all over the world, but with more than half in Eastern Europe. Then great changes came. A third of the entire Jewish people were annihilated by Hitler. Two million returned to Israel.

Few Jews today live where their grandfathers were born. The changes began with the sweep to America at the start of our century. While many German Jews had arrived fifty years earlier, the massive migration was from Czarist Russia after the pogroms of 1903.

Great migrations

We may picture a large Jewish family in a Russian town in 1905, when an early revolution against the Czar had failed.

The Czar's government has used the old trick of turning the impoverished angry peasants against the Jews; drunken mobs have broken into Jewish shops and homes, slaughtering and pillaging. Now the pogrom is over; in this town, luckily, only a few have died. The hidden Torah scrolls have been brought back to the synagogue. Life goes on.

But the Kohansky family, like others, is gathered in conference. There are eight or nine uncles, aunts, many young people, some of whom no longer go to the synagogue— they are "enlightened" and of a socialist turn. One or two are Zionists.

An older son, already married, is deter-

It was in a crowded steerage such as this that the Kohansky uncles would have come to America. Thousands did so in the great tide of immigration that culminated in 1907, the year when Alfred Stieglitz took this photograph.

mined to leave for America. His wife and baby will wait a year, until he saves up enough to send steerage tickets for them. A cousin, unmarried, is determined to go to Palestine. Once and for all the Jews must liberate themselves in their own land. His brother cries No! all mankind must be liberated, and the task of the Jew is to help make a successful revolution right here in Russia. After that, Jews will be completely emancipated, with the peasants and workers!

These two get into a violent dispute and nearly come to blows. They are quieted by grandfather Kohansky, an imposing, old-style Jew with a fine white beard. God protected the whole family, he says. Jews have lived here for centuries, pogroms are storms that pass, Jews have learned to deal with them.

Yes! a younger son cries. In several towns, self-defense units were organized and the pogromists were beaten off! That is the way to do it!

No one changes his mind. Over the next few years, three of the uncles migrate with their families to America. One young man goes to Palestine. A young woman goes to study in Germany. . . . And thus there came enormous population shifts. Would Judaism withstand these three elements, emancipation, enlightenment, and migration?

Migration, Jews had dealt with before. The first great migration to Babylon had stimulated the Judaism of the Rabbis and the Talmud. Would there now be a new development in Judaism? Or would Jews assimilate and Judaism in this "painless" way finally disappear?

Nazism and Communism

It was not assimilation but mass murder that finally caused a third of Jewry to disappear. We should remember that Hitler's plan was for world conquest, that this extermination program would have extended to the Americas as well, had he succeeded.

Destroyed with the bodies of Eastern European Jewry was their way of life. The life of the Yiddish-speaking world, the life of the *shtetl*, already changing under emancipation and enlightenment, was ended.

About three million Russian Jews were just beyond the reach of the invaders, and survived. Whether Judaism can survive among them is another question. Communists teach that religion is the "opium of the people," and they have discouraged the Jewish religion more than any other, to the point where only a few decrepit synagogues remain, attended by a handful of old people, though "Jew" is still stamped on identity cards, and a massive street-participation by young people does take place on the day of Simḥat Torah.

Present-day Jewish populations

At the end of the war there were about ten million Jews left in the world, three million of them in the old East European heartland of Judaism, no longer to be reached. Since the war the world population of Jews has more than half recovered, in numbers, from the act of genocide. There are now 13,400,000

Jews in the world. Instead of Russian Jewry, it is now American Jewry that holds the center. Half of the world Jewish population lives in North and South America, the great majority of these in the United States.

Today the second largest group in numbers remains in Russia, but Israel will in the next few years doubtless occupy second place. But here numbers lose much of their meaning, for while Judaism is barely alive among the Soviets, it has a very special kind of life in Israel.

Aside from Israel, the Soviet Union, and the United States, the largest Jewish populations are in the Argentine, in France, and in England, each around half a million.

The outlook for Judaism

The future of Judaism will depend largely on what happens in the first three countries named. In the U.S.S.R., the future is dark indeed. Certainly nothing creative is taking place. At best, an unknown proportion of Jews are clinging to their spiritual identity. In Israel, there is the profound question of religion and the state, of a national identity or a unifying Judaism, or a combination of both. In the United States, the question of the future of Judaism is posed almost in purity.

There is full emancipation. And there is little from outside to stop a person from ceasing to be a Jew if he wants to discard that identity. There is full enlightenment. Few teachers today would dream of forbidding the reading of "outside" books, even to Orthodox students. And science has made more progress in the last few decades than has been made in the entire previous history of civilization.

It is precisely this growth of study, at first seen as a danger, that can enrich the new phase of Judaism. In the era of the Second Temple and for some time after its destruction, a rich exchange of scholars took place between Jerusalem and Babylon, between the homeland inhabitants of those times and the center of the Diaspora. Such an exchange has begun again in our day. Just as two compilations of Jewish Law were made, the Babylonian Talmud and the Jerusalem Talmud, each in basic harmony with the other, so today's two great centers, in Israel and in the United States, are equally creative in the growing field of Jewish studies.

How do these studies differ from those of the Talmudists?

Modern Jewish scholarship

In previous centuries scholars searched for the legalistic and moralistic explanation of each word in the Bible, particularly in the Books of Moses. If the meaning did not apply to the life around them, they found ways to interpret it to make the law serve.

With enlightenment, another kind of Biblical scholarship developed, and not among Jews alone. The new effort was to understand how and when the different books in the Bible came to be written, and what conditions of life are shown by Mosaic regulations. Modern scholars sought, after decipher-

Dr. Nelson Glueck of the Hebrew Union College–Jewish Institute of Religion, conferring rabbinic ordination. Dr. Glueck's earnest face reflects awareness of the need for dedicated leadership.

ing ancient languages, to search back for the connections to other cultures and to life in those days. Through archaeology, scholars were able to confirm much that was accurate history in the Bible. By learning from digs in Hazor, in Jaffa, in Lachish, in Masada, of the social conditions of those times, they added to our knowledge of the growth of Judaism from a cult to a code of ethics.

The rational spirit

This scholarship, at first feared as antireligious, is now seen to strengthen the rational, modern spirit in its search for the fullest meaning of Judaism. One of our leading authorities, Professor Salo Baron, has said—

If the next generation of American Jews will harbour one hundred truly first-rate scholars, one hundred first-rate writers . . . one hundred first-rate rabbis . . . and one hundred first-rate lay leaders . . . one could look forward confidently to American Judaism's reaching new heights.

Judaism of today, at least outside of Israel, must exist basically on its spiritual quality, on its pure content. After the elimination of altar worship, after the elimination of central authority, after the elimination of forced segregation, even the regulations have largely lost their force, with each Jew who is not strictly Orthodox making his own choice as to what he will observe for the sake of tradition.

So Judaism is now, in a sense, a personally voluntary religion. Now we must study what beliefs such a Judaism embraces and does not embrace.

What do we mean when we say "God"?

8 How do we know there is a God?

Each word in this question can occupy your thoughts for a lifetime, and you might never be satisfied with the answers given by your mind. In the end you might simply say, "Something within me tells me so."

For indeed we may "know" by our minds, by our hearts, or by something else that draws from both mental and emotional sources, the spirit.

Judaism does not insist on any single answer, on any single proof. We can examine some of the ways of knowing, from ancient to modern times. Since the word "we" is in the question, our outlook will be Jewish.

There is a saying that if you ask a Jew a question he will answer with a question; if you ask a Tel Avivian how to get to Herzl Street he will answer, "Why do you want to go to Herzl Street?" So we may first answer with a question about the question itself.

What do we mean by "know"?

Ways of knowing

Scientists tell us that we know something to be true only if we can secure the same results in a controlled experiment under the same conditions. It would be foolish and presumptuous for man to pretend to conduct experiments with God, so the scientists tell us they cannot answer about God.

Philosophers and theologians speak of different kinds of "knowing" about God. The ordinary person can remember that as a child he had no doubt about God. Even before your teachers or parents told you about God you felt His presence. You felt you could speak directly from your heart to God, and quite possibly you still have that feeling.

This is mainly an emotional knowledge. Sometimes it is truer than proved knowledge, even in science, where an intuition, a "hunch" may prove truer than the results of extensive experiments.

A trusting faith

The God who is unquestioningly, directly, known is the God of Abraham, Isaac, and Jacob, because this is the feeling they had about the deity. The Bible tells us how Abraham spoke to God and God replied. Since few of us are able to experience this, we explain that in simpler times people were able to achieve this emotional knowledge more directly.

This trusting faith was imbedded in the Jewish way of life up to modern times. We can see it in a very popular musical play, *Fiddler on the Roof*, drawn from the stories of Sholem Aleichem about Jews who lived a village life in Russia. This play shows us Tevya the milkman, who now and again talks to God. Right straight out of his heart,

Tevya tells God his troubles. Should he let his daughter marry a poor tailor whom she loves, or make her marry a wealthy butcher to whom she is promised? And when a solution comes to Tevya's mind, he says "Thank you, God," for the answer.

Some call this a naive idea of God. Others say we may feel we know God as we know other beings in our life, but on a higher plane; God is a "thou" instead of a "you." Such is the relationship to God that is explained by the great philosopher Martin Buber, who developed his beliefs from his studies of Ḥasidism. The Ḥasidim believed that God is aware of man, that we know God because God knows us, and as Martin Buber put it, that a "dialogue" between man and God can be attained. Surely to receive an answer is the proof that there is a God!

Prayers of the Ḥasid

The Ḥasidim believed that God sometimes does intervene in human affairs. Today, after the holocaust in Europe, we find this difficult to believe; still, in the prime of the Ḥasidim, there were constant pogroms and other grave troubles for the Jews, and yet they felt God sometimes intervened. Today as well, this Jewish religious movement having survived the holocaust, feels secure in this faith. Sometimes, as they picture it, the way to God is blocked by the dense cloud of evil that man creates on earth, but an overwhelming effort of goodness, an intensity of true prayer, can clear the path. There is mysticism in their approach to knowledge of God, but they believe that the natural order of the universe can sometimes be changed, altered at the will of God, in response to humanity. The pure, heartfelt prayers of a *Tzaddik*, or of a child, may pierce the clouds of evil.

There are Ḥasidic legends that show the intense effort to understand the meaning of Godly intervention. One tale tells of a young bride who died on her wedding day, and how the Baal Shem Tov himself ascended to heaven and pleaded that the order of the universe be changed so that she might be allowed to live and fulfill her marriage with her destined love. "Only for the sake of uniting predestined lovers," the tale ends, "may the order of the universe be altered." What, then, is meant by the phrase "predestined lovers"? It appears of itself to imply a *kind* of order. Did these two bear a natural relationship to each other, and is the plan of all creation organized, even to the union of every human couple? We may well ask this, since a Talmudic legend tells us that God Himself makes marriages, and teaches that human beings should not arrogate to themselves the right of making such decisions for others.

If we look further into this Ḥasidic story we find that there had indeed been interference with the normal marriage plans. The bride's late aunt had been the first wife of this bridegroom. And on her deathbed she had extracted from these two the promise that they would never be married to each other. In this meaningful tale, it was the spirit of the dead woman, jealous beyond the grave, that had claimed the life of her niece when she and her prospective bridegroom were found to be forsaking their deathbed promise.

What decisions, then, are embodied in the Baal Shem's intervention against death, or in God's intervening in response to his prayer? First, that life goes on. Life belongs to the living, and the dead hand of the past cannot block it. And the promise? It was made under duress, to allay the anguish of a dying woman. And having been made under duress it was not morally binding or valid under Jewish law. (Just so, we have the most touching Yom Kippur prayer, the solemn Kol Nidre of Spanish Jews who had been forced by the Inquisition to convert to Christianity, and who cried out in their secret Jewish observances that all vows—*Kol Nidre* —they had made, meaning the vows of conversion imposed on them, were unbinding and void.)

Also, if God, the First Cause, is spiritual, and a jealous God—jealous of His order and power—what business has a petty mortal spirit of jealousy and spite in interfering with His destiny for man? Or, we might ask, what false sense of guilt is leading this prospective bride to break the Second Commandment and bow down to the "spirit" of a dead mortal? Who's in charge here?

In short, we see that even this tale of mystical overthrowing of the "order of the universe" is in itself actually a plea for God's pre-established order of life and love and reasonableness. The prayer of the Tzaddik, in Ḥasidic belief, had pierced the enshrouding clouds of evil—superstition and fear and self-blame—that came between

Here in Israel the joy of Simḥat Torah is being celebrated in the Ḥasidic tradition.

man and his sense of the Godhead. And the verdict from the Throne was for life.

We may say that the Ḥasidim believed that all destiny is already worked out by God's will, and that even the laws of nature can sometimes be set aside in order to fulfill that destiny. This belief may be linked to the Biblical story of the angels visiting Abraham and Sarah, to tell them that a child will yet be born to them. They were astonished, for Sarah had passed the time when a woman may conceive a child. Yet the way of nature was not final, and she gave birth to Isaac.

Demands of the intellect

Thus, from Abraham to the Ḥasidim, Jews felt they knew God, and that proof of God came when the rules of nature were occasionally altered at His will. But their faith came before the "proof"; their way of knowing God exists was from within themselves. The intellect asks for another kind of proof. Myths and miracles are set aside in favor of logic.

As we have seen with Maimonides, the logical mind traces back cause and effect, and comes to the idea of God as the "First Cause."

When we see how cells live and multiply, when we see how atoms combine in their patterns, we realize that everything proceeds by cause and effect. Thus everything can be traced back to the first cause. But what was the first cause? What was the spirit that moved in the void and set an orderly universe into being? What started the one-celled amoeba on the course of evolution?

Logically we know God exists because there has to have been a first cause. But suppose man may yet analyze out the universal clockwork, man may yet solve the entire mechanics of creation; will not the first cause also be revealed? But hasn't it already been revealed? In Judaism this is called God.

The power for good

Suppose the physical universe, all creation, is ongoing and cannot be altered. Suppose even what we regard as our God-given free will is in fact enslaved by hidden causes. Suppose even that God is not aware of man.

Still, there is a way of thinking, explained by Rabbi Mordecai Kaplan, that brings us back to a knowledge of God. In this way of thinking, God is quite simply defined as the power that makes for good. That power exists, for each of us feels it all the time in his conscience. Godhead, then, is "all the relationships, tendencies and agencies which in their totality go to make human life worthwhile in the deepest and most abiding sense."

Is this still Judaism? Is this still the God of Abraham, Isaac, and Jacob, of Moses and Maimonides and Einstein? If we look back to the story of creation, we find the days of creation ending with the words, "and He saw that it was good."

This goodness is not only a moral idea, a satisfaction for doing right instead of wrong. It is the good feeling that comes in the presence of beauty, of animal life, of forests, snow, of human skill. If life were merely mechanical, why should we feel any such exhilaration? This is the feeling the artist has when he completes a poem, a sculpture. At a certain moment he knows it is done and cannot be changed. He feels godly.

This may again be called an anthropomorphic way of explaining God. We are limited by human limitations. Judaism tells us we cannot ever know God completely; we must use what understanding there is within us. We do not create God in the image of man, but we try to reach out with that unexplained feeling of goodness within ourselves, to goodness in the great Unexplainable.

Three approaches

There are, then, three ways of knowing there is God, and each is an approach.

We may know from the heart. The philosopher-scholar Hugo Bergman tells us, "The believer encounters God. He knows God's hand is extended to him. He speaks to God and receives an answer. He prays to Him, being just as certain of His existence as he is of his own or that of his neighbor. He cannot offer objective evidence for what, in his heart, he knows to be utterly true and real."

We may know from the mind. Maimonides tells us that God is an abstract principle of being. God so far transcends human comprehension that all positive descriptions of Him are inappropriate.

Others prove God through the mind, in the very fact that God exists to us as an idea.

The philosopher Hermann Cohen said, "As an idea, He cannot be described nor does He have to be believed in. He can be discovered by the process of reason itself."

Those who want to "disprove" God also turn to God as an idea, saying that God is an idea invented by man. "Man created God in his own image," they insist, giving God human feelings such as anger and pity and satisfaction in goodness. Thus they turn around the Biblical view that God created man in His own image.

All of these intellectual debates may seem to turn in circles, but in the end they tell us that man's mind is not able in itself to complete the idea, or the "proof" of God. The heart's proof of God is "I feel Him," and the mind's proof of God, conversely, is "He is beyond me."

We may know God through the soul, or spirit. Rabbi Leo Baeck, of Berlin, whom the Nazis put into the concentration camp of Theresienstadt, and who survived, wrote in *The Essence of Judaism:*

Certain thinkers have . . . maintained, that the idea of God is in itself no more religious than, say, the idea of gravitation . . . For it is possible to accept the existence of a God on philosophical grounds to explain the cosmic order by establishing a first cause in the process of nature. . . . The philosophical formula of God as the first mover is in itself not really richer in religious significance than any other philosophical idea. In this idea faith can find neither its basis nor strength. The gift of religious certainty is conveyed solely by that which God means to our existence and our soul, by the inner consist-

*"Holy, holy, holy is the Lord of hosts."
So spoke the prophet Isaiah, striving
to convey his sense of direct
awareness of God.*

ency which our life thus gains, by our resultant moral power . . . that feeling which realizes the call from God to us each day of our lives: "Where art thou?" . . . whether we approach God with devout words of intimacy or we desire to approach God by pure thought, the result is essentially the same so long as we feel that He is our God.

The spark of conscience

Perhaps the closest one-word "proof" of God in Judaism is the conscience. Our religious laws, social rules, wisdom rules, laws of justice, all are efforts to guide and train our sense of right and wrong. This "still small voice" is the godliness that some believe is the image of God in man. Not the tongue, not the eye of God, not any physical attribute, but the power that moves us, conscience itself.

And conscience is in harmony with the prophetic spirit, the "word of God," which is the core of Jewish ethics, and of the great process of life. Rabbi Kaplan feels that this very process itself is God. "Since God is life, knowledge, goodness—what else can He be but a process?"

The spark of God that is in each of us, our conscience, knows in itself the direction of that process toward good, just as birds know the direction for their migration. This sense of a spirit in man (Job 32:8), an element within ourselves that can be in harmony with the total spirit of which it is a part, is perhaps our best way of knowing there is a God, and of knowing God.

The knowledge within us

Through this spirit, we in ourselves can change, by striving to put ourselves in harmony with what we know is right. The prophets were already expressing this by arousing people to listen to their conscience.

In the end, all the proofs and explanations are only words that give emphasis to the knowledge of God that we already have within us.

In *Basic Judaism*, Milton Steinberg said, "Affirming God, Judaism permits considerable latitude as to conceptions of Him. It allows the individual to decide whether He is to be envisaged as transcendent or immanent, whether as an abstract principle of being as with Maimonides and the Kabbalistic mystics, or, what is more common, as supremely personal."

Let us remember the famous parable about Rabbi Joshua ben Ḥananya and the Emperor Hadrian, who wanted to behold the Jewish God. "That is impossible," the Rabbi said, and he bade the Emperor look into the sun. "I cannot," the Emperor answered. Then the Rabbi said, "How much more beyond your power must it be to look at God Himself?"

Man's ignorance of God, our tradition tells us, is greater than his knowledge of God. "Yet our ignorance of God," Rabbi Steinberg wrote, ". . . is not total. If the knowledge we have of Him is not equal to our curiosity, it is adequate for our needs."

But it is adequate only if it is extended in a constant lifelong search.

9 Does God punish wrong and reward goodness?

From the very story of creation in the Bible, our Scriptures keep telling us how God punishes wrong. Sometimes we are also shown how goodness is rewarded, but the greater concern of our forefathers seems to have been to keep from doing wrong—through fear of heavenly punishment.

The teaching of obedience

Students of the Bible, while agreeing that much of it is inspired, also have shown that many stories were included to teach certain points. Those who fashioned our Bible through ages of telling and retelling, selected and shaped this material in a moral way.

The very story of Adam and Eve is a story of punishment for doing wrong. The first sin in the Bible is disobedience.

Isn't this what one first teaches a child? The need for obedience?

Again we see that the development of Judaism is like the development of man.

The idea of punishments and rewards

After teaching obedience to God, just as one teaches a child to obey the parent, the Bible then goes on to teach the great rules of human society. In the story of Cain and Abel comes the punishment for murder.

Then there is teaching on the side of goodness. In the covenant of God with Abraham, we are told of a reward for goodness, for obedience: If Abraham will be obedient to God, he and his seed will be rewarded by being given the land that lies before Abraham, and by increase and protection.

Stories of the punishment of an entire people for going bad, for worshiping idols, for all kinds of evil-doing, also come to us from our earliest times. The flood is explained as a punishment for evil-doing; all mankind is to be erased, and God will start over, as it were, with only Noah's family, and one pair of each kind of creature. Later we have the story of Sodom in which, again, an evil population is wiped out.

These teachings are followed by the teachings of the prophets, outcries telling how God will use invaders to punish the wrong-doing of the Jews. But also, from the time of Abraham and on through the prophets, there is a strain of creative goodness, a value that exists regardless of the fear of punishment, but simply for itself.

The thoughts of reward and punishment remain dominant. In early Judaism, God was seen as directly involved with what happened on earth. He was aware of each happening and He could and did intervene.

The need for deeper explanations

We may see this today as the "policeman" idea of God. And it was not long before

Fleeing the destruction of Sodom, Lot's wife looked back and was turned into a "pillar of salt." These pinnacles on the mountain of Sodom contain a salt bed 150 feet thick.

Judaism grew up to the point where a broader conception was needed. For even in early days—just as now—people could recognize that in life it is quite often the good who suffer, whereas the immoral, the unscrupulous, seem to have all the rewards, riches and power and even honor. So the evidence of human life often contradicted moral preaching. One way to explain this was to say that God would reward good people in the world to come, in heaven, while the evil people would be punished by never being allowed to come into the presence of God. They would go to hell, the opposite of heaven, and be punished in a fiery *Gehenna.*

This idea of heaven and hell is not a dogma, or an absolute part of Judaism. Ideas of heavenly rewards and hellish punishment in an afterlife are part of the absolute teaching of some other religions, although in Judaism these same ideas are left to personal belief or disbelief.

In Christianity and in the Muslim faith, for example, what happens in the afterlife is part of a system of belief. Yet our credo of Maimonides, in the Middle Ages, already leaves out belief in heaven and hell. Still, our religious literature is filled with such tales as illustrations of right and wrong.

Tales from the Talmud

Here is a tale from the time when the Talmud was being written, which corresponds to the early days of Christianity. And the tale shows us the belief, in that time, in the heavenly reward for good behavior.

The story pictures heaven, in which the saintly scholars, some of them yet to be born on earth, are seated close around God, studying the holy Torah, just like good pupils in a ḥeder. Since eternity reigns, there is no before and after, and everything that is yet to be is already known to these pure spirits.

When Moses went up to God, the rabbinical tale tells us, he found God sitting and putting little crowns atop the letters of the Torah. Moses asked God for whose sake He was putting such crowns on the letters of the Torah. God replied "A man is to appear on earth, many generations from now, Akiva ben Joseph by name, and for each tip of every letter of the Torah he will expound beautiful rulings."

Impressed, Moses asked, "I would like to see this wonderful person," and God replied, "Turn around." Moses did, and saw a group of enthralled students listening to Rabbi Akiva. So Moses found a seat among them in the eighth row. He could hardly follow Rabbi Akiva's brilliant exposition, nor could all of the students, for one of them asked Akiva for proof of a certain teaching. "That is a teaching which was delivered to Moses on Mount Sinai. No further proof is needed," Akiva said.

Moses went back to God and remarked, "Thou hast a man like this, and Thou givest the Torah through me?" Then God said, "Be silent: thus it has seemed good to Me." Then Moses said, "Thou hast shown me his knowledge of the Torah. Now show me his reward."

Once more God said, "Turn around." Moses did so, and he saw the flesh of Akiva being stripped off him with a butcher's pole, after the Romans had flayed him alive. Then Moses said, "Such is his knowledge of the Torah, and thus is his reward?" And God said, "Silence. So it has seemed good to Me."

This powerful though gruesome story shows us how the wisdom teachers of the early days of Judaism tried to deal with the unanswerable question of the punishment of the good. Even Moses, the story shows us, was baffled and upset, but, though protesting, he accepted the idea that what seemed wrong on earth would be balanced out in heaven where Akiva would return for eternity.

Every man has some good and some evil in him, and the Talmudic Rabbis suggested that a good man might be punished on earth for his few evil mistakes, before receiving his reward, which was far more consequential in heaven. Thus, Rabbi Akiva had made the mistake of declaring Bar Kokhba to be the Messiah, and encouraging the Jews to follow him. For this, Akiva was caught and brutally executed by the Romans. And then he went up to heaven to resume his perfect existence.

A simpler story relates this idea for the ordinary man. It tells of a pious person and a wicked tax collector who lived in Ashkelon. Both died; the pious man went alone to his grave while the tax collector was honored by a procession of the whole town. A scholar pondered, why was the wicked man honored and the pious man neglected?

He then had a dream in which he saw that the pious man had once committed a sin by putting his *Tefillin* on in reverse order, the head before the hand. He also saw that

This eighteenth-century engraving of the Tefillin shows the Shel Yad *as worn on the left arm facing the heart, and the* Shel Rosh *which is placed in the center of the forehead.*

the tax collector had once done a good deed in walking through the market place; he had dropped a loaf of bread. A beggar had snatched it up, and the owner had not claimed it back. Even though it was out of shame that he had let the beggar keep the bread, this was still a good deed. So each had received his due on earth, the pious man for his absent-minded sin, and the rich man for his unintended good deed. But in heaven?

The scholar had a second dream and saw the pious Jew walking in paradise under shady trees, and drinking from wells of sweet water, while the tax collector lay near the brink of a river with his tongue hanging out, and try as he might, he could not reach the water.

These tales show us that, to balance the injustice that man witnesses on earth, he can believe in reward in an afterlife. Thus, Jews could keep their faith in God's justice. In this form of balancing the scales, a belief in heaven and in an afterlife was necessary. We may accept that belief or we may see the whole explanation as poetic.

Repentance and reform

Our wisdom literature also taught that God, in punishing evil, forgave the repentant. And here we begin to see the place of conscience in Judaism.

The Ḥasidim, too, believe strongly in reward in heaven. On the subject of repentance, they cherish the saying of Rabbi Schmelke:

He who regrets his transgressions may do so for two reasons: one, that he stands in the fear of punishment; the other, that he is contrite for having displeased his beloved Father in heaven. In the first instance, the sin becomes suspended, but a record of it remains. In the second, the sin is completely erased and no trace of it remains, as if no sin had ever been committed.

In other words, sincere respect of God, which we may say is the conscience-wish to do right, is better than mere fear of punishment.

Another wise Ḥasidic saying about repentance is that of Rabbi Bunam, who was asked, "How can a man know if his repentance is genuine?" The Rabbi answered, "If he loses the desire to commit these same offenses again."

Repentance through fear of punishment depends on belief in a God who is aware of the actions of man, who may, and does, interfere. But the desire to do right is a psychologic reaction. It may still be seen as instilled by God, as a way for us to carry out His judgment.

Conscience and self-punishment

Suppose we question the idea of a God who is aware of the actions of man, aware of every deed and thought in every single human being? Suppose we feel that such a personification of God is not satisfactory to all of us? Suppose we feel that the experiences of our daily existence do not let us believe in this "policeman" idea of God, especially when He does not act, as in the holocaust? And yet we feel that in some way goodness is rewarded, and evil is punished.

In what way? Modern psychology tells us about self-punishment. Indeed we are told that some of us often feel too guilty about our bad deeds, and punish ourselves in unrealized ways, so much that we become examples of masochism. This is a question for rigorous self-examination, but the basic idea of self-punishment, of self-regulation, of inward recognition of our bad deeds, is godly. It is part of the idea of God's immanence, or presence within us, through our spirit or conscience.

This concept does not go contrary to Judaism in Biblical times or in the times of Maimonides. It is rather a continuation of Judaism in new ways consistent with science, perhaps only new ways of saying things. This method allows us to drop the idea of God the bookkeeper, with rewards postponed for the afterlife. Though we believe in God, we may say that we simply do not know about an afterlife. We may even say that we do not believe that God intervenes directly in human affairs.

Though some good Jews will argue passionately against this, others will argue passionately for it. All this is in the area of human uncertainty, and its uncovering may be part of the great process of life.

Whichever side we take in that argument, in every form of Judaism there remains the moral idea that in some way or other, goodness is rewarded and evil is punished. Goodness may be rewarded, for those who believe in heaven, in the afterlife. It may be rewarded, psychologically, within ourselves. And, as is commonly said, goodness is its own reward.

This saying may have special meaning for those who feel, in accordance with Jewish teaching, that man lives in a partnership with God. One of the worst results of doing wrong may be that it disrupts a person's sense of fulfilling his rightful place and function in God's scheme of things, for the Torah is closely tied to the Jewish sense of order and harmony in God's universe.

An inner force for good

A story of a boy's life in Harlem shows us how an inner desire to be decent and good, without being in the least goody-goody, overcame a criminal environment. *Manchild in the Promised Land,* by Claude Brown, tells of a childhood in which brutality, theft, drug-taking, and prostitution were the normal content of life. The code under which the author lived was totally antisocial, yet the book is pervaded by an inner kindness of spirit, pity, love for his people, so many of whom—including his own little brother —fell victim to drug addiction. From one church, from one religious cult to another, this young man sought for something to believe in. Finally he worked out a creative life through his own innate sense of what is right, what is good. This boy made it, through extraordinary force of character. In a sense he found his own religion within himself, and one can only think of it as some essential force of godliness. It is interesting that another Negro, Sammy Davis, Jr., found that the teachings of Judaism were of help to him in his own crisis. In a sense Judaism is an organized system of experience, old as civilization, helping our divinely inspired sense of right.

Agreement on right and wrong

Modern and traditional Judaism may differ on how to describe God. The modernist tries to stay within the borders of science and philosophy. When he uses examples from the traditional sources, he feels they are poetic. They may have more truth in their perceptions than science has yet achieved. He accepts such aspects of Judaism as vision, as poetry, sometimes as superstition, and tries to carry the insight into his own way of thinking, his own way of worship.

When it comes to deciding what is wrong and what is right, outside of the areas of ritual, both types of Jew are almost certain to agree. So will people from other religions adhering to the great moral codes. And they too will emphasize that punishment for doing wrong takes place through our own conscience, quite aside from what may or may not happen in an afterworld.

Atonement and forgiveness

Through having created the conscience within man, God, without intervening in each case, punishes us for our evil deeds. And only when we have satisfied our own conscience, through repentance or deeds of

The shofar, sounded to usher in the High Holy Days, calls Jews all over the world to consider their lives and consciences, to reflect upon the lessons of the old year, and prepare themselves for the new.

atonement, or changing ourselves, can we feel released. An essay by Hayim Greenberg shows us this point through another Talmudic story:

An ugly sin had been committed by Rabbi Eleazar ben Durdia, and he had lost his place in the world to come. The sinner went out to the valley between the mountains and cried aloud, "Valley and mountains, beg forgiveness for me!" But they answered, "How can we beg forgiveness for you since we need forgiveness for ourselves?" (This alone is an interesting thought, for it suggests that in our tradition nature too can sin.) The remorseful Rabbi then turned to the heavens and earth, to the sun and to the moon, to the stars and to the planets, but all gave him the same answer. At last he turned to himself. "It all depends on me—no mediator, neither priest nor saint, not even the entire universe can win mercy and forgiveness for me, only I myself!" He sat down and lowered his head between his knees and wept until his soul departed from him. At once a voice from heaven called out, "Rabbi Eleazer ben Durdia is ready for the life hereafter!" He had been given back his place in the world to come, and even, as the Talmud notes, his title of Rabbi.

We see that even when heavenly intervention came, in this case, it acted through the conscience of man. And to guide us, so that we may not take any willful set of ideas or ideologies, any fanatic creed as a license for so-called "acts of conscience," we have the Torah.

The whole tradition of Judaism helps us in the understanding of right and wrong that is contained in our conscience. If we want personally to believe that by this means God punishes wrong and rewards goodness, we are fully within what Judaism teaches.

But is all wrong punished, all goodness rewarded? What of people of whom we feel, "They have no conscience?"

Perhaps they are part of the abundant evidence that God's world is as yet very far from reaching perfection, and that God has given man the task of developing a universal conscience.

10   Does God answer prayers?

If God may not even be aware of man, what is the use of praying?

If God is aware of man but will not interfere with what happens, what is the use of praying?

We have seen that in Judaism there remain differing explanations for the ways of God. First, there is the traditional belief that God is aware of man and can at His will change the order of the universe for extraordinary reasons. Those who believe that this is true also believe that God can answer prayers directly.

Problems of unanswered prayer

It would seem that this traditional belief in a God who responds is the only one that gives a purpose to prayer. Yet the danger is that this brings us close to superstition. And when prayer seems unanswered, it can bring us to disappointment and even to atheism. For we ask ourselves, where was the God that could not—or worse, would not—respond to the prayers of all the innocent concentrated in the death camps of the Nazis?

86

And where is the God that does not respond to the prayers that still rise up from all the human fields of slaughter, since there is war without end in the world?

And this leads us back to a God who does not interfere, sometimes called a self-limiting God.

Yet all Jewish belief in God agrees that God's ultimate purpose is justice, whether by interfering, or by waiting for man to perfect himself. Whether He is an infinite being, a process, or an idea, His purpose is justice. And every way of thinking about God also agrees in the value of prayer. As to an "answer" to prayer, this is almost as difficult to explain as God Himself.

To understand what we mean by an answer we must be clear about what we mean by prayer.

Prayers of petition

The simplest idea of a prayer is a wish.

We know of the childish or primitive wish for good things to happen, for gifts that will not "cost" God anything, but will give us joy, for happiness that need not be harmful to anyone. "O God," the child says, "let there be a nice sunny day for my birthday party. It really makes no difference to You, so let it be nice." And the parents tell the child not to bother God with selfish prayers; to save them for something important.

But the weather is very important to the farmer, so important that in our traditional prayers Jews in all lands still petition for dew at the season when it is needed in Israel.

And what happens when two people, equally deserving, pray for the opposite thing? Our Rabbis pondered over this problem. What about a prayer for rain that would be helpful to one man's crops but would be harmful by flooding the fields of another?

The tale of Honi, the rain maker

There is fun-poking at this kind of prayer in the story the early Rabbis told of Honi the Circle-Drawer, a famous rain maker of his day, and as his name tells us, a kind of magician. The month of Adar had passed and no rain had fallen. People appealed to Honi. He drew a circle around himself and recited from the prophet Habakkuk. "Master of the World! I swear by Thy Great Name that I will not move from this circle until Thou showest mercy to Thy children!" Rain began to trickle. But the people complained that Honi had brought down enough rain to free him from the circle, yet not enough for the crops. So Honi tried again. "Not for such rain did I pray," he sang out, "but for rain sufficient to fill the cisterns, ditches, and caves."

Rain came pouring down, "each drop as big as the opening of a barrel."

That was too much. The villagers cried, "This rain will destroy the world!" The Circle-Drawer sought to temper the flood. "Not for such rain did I pray, but for a rain of benevolence, blessing, and graciousness," he intoned. Whereupon the heavenly faucet was at last turned down to proper measure. Yet as the streets were deep in mud, Honi's clients said, "Just as thou hast prayed for rain to come, so pray now that it should stop."

Before he bothered the Almighty any more, Honi thought it wise to make a sacrifice, so he asked that they bring him a bullock. The Circle-Drawer laid both his hands on the sacrifice and intoned, "Master of the world! Thy people Israel can stand neither too much good, nor too much punishment; when Thou becamest wroth. withholding rain, they could not endure it; now let it be Thy will that there be ease in the world!" Immediately the wind blew, the clouds dispersed, and the sun began to shine. The people went out into the fields and brought home mushrooms.

Nevertheless, poor Honi was scolded by Rabbi Shimon ben Sheṭaḥ for profaning the name of God with all his back-and-forth requests. But finally, as Honi was a well-meaning soul, he was forgiven. After all, he had only wanted good for the people.

This story tells us three things: First, that in Honi's days many Jews did believe that prayer can bring God to alter the course of nature. Others made fun of this idea. Secondly, the story tells us that Jews also believed that certain persons can help others, through having a direct "prayer line." And finally it tells us that Judaism taught that a brazen use of prayer was "taking the name of the Lord in vain."

Lingering magical feelings

Yet the human desire for help in this baffling world makes it difficult for us even now to overcome these early magical feelings that still persist in us, the feeling that God can be flattered, perhaps bribed, or that some better person may have "a pipeline" to God. Examples of superstitious prayer are found in all religions. Perhaps the strangest is the Tibetan prayer wheel, in which requests are written on bits of paper attached to a wheel, which the monks keep whirling, as though by this means the words will fly up to heaven.

In Israel we may see certain shrines like the Cave of Elijah near Haifa, or the grave of Rabbi Simeon ben Yoḥai at Meron, where believers deposit their prayer messages. And don't we put little prayer notes into the chinks of the Temple Wall in Jerusalem?

Personal and communal prayers

The legends of the Ḥasidim are rich with stories of the results of the prayers of the Baal Shem Tov and other great Rabbis. Women who are barren come to the Rabbi, that he may pray for them to have a child, and a child is born. But beyond such personal petitions, we reach to intense, communal prayers, that pogroms may end, that the suffering of the whole people may be halted, that the Messiah may come down and bring peace on earth. And the *Tzaddikim* "ascend" in such prayers. We are told of vigils and long fasts, of purifications, and of such intensity of prayer that the soul leaves the body to make its supplication in the heavens and almost fails to find its way back.

The idea of asking a "purer person" to

Pious Jews pray at the outer portion of the Western Wall, the remains of the external portion of Herod's Temple, destroyed with the fall of Jerusalem.

pray for us is rather natural. Our tradition tells us, "A man shall not approach God while the spoil of the poor is hidden in his household, or seek forgiveness for transgressions with the design of sinning again as soon as his prayers are done."

And also, an innocent soul, an unlearned person, an ordinary person of good intent, may still feel that he does not have the ingress to the Almighty of a learned Jew, a rabbi, or a *tzaddik*.

Thus, prayer is surrounded with moral purpose.

The Talmud tells us, "Whoever has it in his power to pray for his neighbor and fails to do so, is called a sinner . . . [another kind of "sin of omission"] Whoever prays on behalf of a fellow man while himself in need of the same thing, will be answered first."

Just as a man should use prayer to help his neighbor, he must not use prayer to turn away trouble from himself if it may then fall on a neighbor. A man who hears a fire alarm ringing should not pray that the fire is in someone else's house. Besides, the Talmud says, the fire is already where it is, and a man should not pray against what is already a fact.

In the same way, with a more happy example, a man whose wife is about to bear a baby should not pray that it be a boy or a girl, for the unborn child is already a boy or a girl.

Formal prayers of worship

Thus we see that traditional Judaism on principle avoids asking God to change the

Chaim Nachman Bialik was the author of many fine stories and stirring poems, as well as beautiful prayers.

order of the universe. Such prayer is reserved for the most extraordinary of causes. Actually the great body of our prayer is worship; our most wonderful prayers express praise of the Almighty, thanks, awe, and humility. They avoid bargaining, wheedling, or begging. Prayers of worship are answered by a sense of peace, or at times of elation.

In the traditional prayer book, or a more modern version such as that of the Reconstructionists, we will find that the prayers for our use on Sabbath, on the holidays, as well as the prayers that the pious Jew repeats three times a day, are mostly poems of praise. If they are prayers of supplication, they ask that we may be made better people, that there be peace and goodness in the world.

Even so, many persons feel a resistance to prayers that are already written and set out for them. This is often called "rote prayer." It cannot be denied that rote prayer may have in it something of the feeling of magic incantation. We all know how sad and ridiculous it is to watch people racing through prayers as though they will satisfy God by repeating these words with their lips. Our own tradition tells us that true prayer must come from the heart.

But there is also a reason for the formal prayer. These prayers contain poetry from the religious genius of King David, Yehudah ha-Levi, Ibn Gabirol, and other great Jewish spirits. Another reason is unity with our community. Man is a social being; he is uncertain of himself, he needs the comfort of his family, his people around him and in accord with him, and thus worship is practiced in groups. There, with the community, we establish our sense of our place in God's order, in relation to our fellowmen, each strengthened by the others, taking within himself some of their burdens as they share in his. The Jewish tradition of the *minyan*, of ten men to say the *kaddish* together, is an example.

Private prayer

Our tradition also recognizes that prayer is deeply private at times, that man's relationship to God is the most intimate part of his being, and therefore he prays alone whenever the spirit moves him, and he often seems to be praying alone even when he is in a crowded synagogue. Visitors to old-fashioned synagogues are often astounded at the seeming discord. Each man starts when he chooses, interrupts his prayers for a chat, or perhaps turns away from all others. Suddenly all are very quiet, mumbling to themselves, shaking their heads to send off anyone who may approach. They are repeating the silent Eighteen Benedictions.

Our prayer books

Some of our thinkers and religious leaders feel that the entire content and manner of Jewish prayer must be renewed. They feel the prayer books should be changed. Rabbi Milton Steinberg pointed out that the *Mahzor* and all our prayers reflect the environ-ment and civilization of the times in which they were composed. Are the needs still the same today?

Though the values underlying the Mahzor are eternal, even eternal values have to clothe themselves with the flesh in order to appeal to those to whom they are addressed. The Talmud tells us, "Better a few prayers with devotion than many prayers without devotion."

Our prayers no longer fire the imagination. Constant repetition of such phrases as King of the universe, Lord, Master, constant praise and flattery with strings of words like resplendent, glorious, almighty, do not express the depth that man seeks in his relationship to God. God does not need to be told how great and wonderful He is!

Rabbi Steinberg suggests that a revision of prayers be carried out not by rabbis alone, but with laymen. "The more learned the rabbis," he adds, "the less satisfactory will be the version."

The effects of prayers

But what is the object of these regular sessions of prayer? Whatever the version used, they ask for no specific answer as a rule, but speak for a general good relationship to God, a peace and betterment for ourselves, through being a God-thinking community. Prayer of this kind is answered in its effect on ourselves, on our constant awareness of seeking a better way of life.

Whether a prayer is spoken in unity with others or in the solitude in our own heart, can it still avail if we are among those Jews who do not believe that God is aware of man, or that God will by one iota change the order of the universe?

One way of understanding the value of prayer is to consider that we really pray to, or into, the God-given spirit within ourselves. If we think of God as a vast spiritual conception, beyond all, we still believe that creation is a part of God, and that a "spark" of godliness is in the soul of each person. Thus, the prayer addressed to the Godhead is always a prayer heard by that divine spark, the conscience within ourselves.

Doing one's part

In this way, those who believe that God is not aware in the same sense that a human being is aware, still somehow believe that through ourselves awareness exists in Him. For man's freedom of will enables him to a considerable extent to choose or change his own actions. Even when natural obstacles or human obstacles are too powerful for a man to overcome, he can strive to change his own inner attitude toward those overpowering happenings. Thus an inward prayer may make a man more resolute in the face of a storm, and it may help him to retain his own sense of morality even if he has to take part in a war.

This aspect of prayer was described by the late Zionist leader, the thinker Hayim Greenberg, who wrote—

If a man's prayer is genuine and offered in sincerity, it has an effect, first of all, upon himself. He cannot alter the Cosmic Order by his prayer, he cannot break through the chain of law and necessity that binds natural events and bring about a miracle, but he can integrate, or reintegrate, himself in the general scheme of existence and events, and thus obtain succor for his need. If a man's legs have been amputated he knows quite well that no matter how much he may pray, new legs will not grow on the stumps. But prayer may give him the strength to live in harmony (or in greater harmony) with himself and with the world, even without legs. Through prayer he has the power to . . . achieve a state of reconciliation with his fate. Through prayer he may sometimes discover in himself such hidden or dormant sources of delight and gratitude for his very existence as will greatly compensate him for his loss.

One of the aspects of prayer, undoubtedly, is just this turning to oneself, this navigation of the depths of one's own so largely unexplored soul, this discovery of strata of our own being with which there is hardly any contact in daily, diffuse living. Traditional believers, too, whether they know it or not, pray not only to God but to themselves as well. Prayer to oneself is certainly answered, more often than we may imagine. There are (and have been through the ages) thousands of trustworthy, living witnesses to testify to that. Everyone of us, at bottom, is potentially his own witness to it. . . .

There may be the danger here of a kind of self-deification. But what is meant is contained quite simply in such a prayer as "God, make me a better person." For the conscience of God within each of us shows us how to be better, and we have been given the will to choose what is right.

The tradition of Judaism also insists to us that prayer does not replace human effort. One should not pray to God and sit back and wait for the wish to come true. A sick man calls on God but also on his physician. Otherwise, our sages tell us, he is a sinner against his own soul and against God who endowed the physician with skill and the drugs with their healing properties.

A high form of worship

The Talmud declares, "prayer is greater than sacrifice." This was a landmark of the advance of Judaism from a primitive to a higher form of worship.

Every form of Judaism includes the belief that prayers are somehow to some degree answered. Jews may disagree as to how they are answered. Jews may disagree as to the form of prayer. Some may not believe that prayer can be delegated to "saintly persons." The Jew who is against ritual may believe that prayer has only a psychological effect within himself. But still, prayer is a release for anguish, to which even the most sophisticated person turns almost automatically.

Prayer helps us to find our deeper selves, our deeper will. The more traditional Jew believes that we do, through prayer, put ourselves into relationship with God, that He is aware of each of us, that regular prayer confirms our daily, constant presence before God. He believes that divine intervention can come in answer to prayer but that if it does not come, a higher cause keeps God from answering. The less traditional Jew believes that God as a power does not intervene, but that prayer can be answered in many ways through changes in ourselves, by each person's own kind of faith.

Worshipers at weekday morning prayer services in Israel wear the Tallit and Tefillin. The long earlocks distinguish the young Ḥasidic boy.

11 Why do we suffer?

We all know that there are good and evil impulses in man. Our tradition explained this in the terms *yetzer ha-tov* and *yetzer ha-ra,* the urge to good and the urge to evil. And we know that between these moral poles in ourselves there is a constant current; there is a word for this push-and-pull, this tension of life—it is *dialectic*. Through this dialectic, this alternating current between good and bad impulses, each person's character is formed.

For example, a schoolmate's *yetzer ha-ra* may prompt him to ask you for the answer to an examination question. Your *yetzer ha-ra* may suggest that you give it to him. He is your friend, isn't he? And he needs help? Your *yetzer ha-tov* will counter with the reminder that it is more fair to all who abide by the school rules, that you should not tell him the answer. Your *yetzer ha-ra* will come back and say that no one will ever know, and that even his parents will feel bad if he brings home a poor grade.

At this point, you may stop and ask what is his highest good—and yours, assuming that you love a neighbor as yourself. The same push-and-pull motivations may take place in deciding whether to go along with "the bunch" in the fad of swiping something from the five-and-ten, or in trying an "innocent" drug. In the first instance, the common case of an exam, your *yetzer ha-tov* may argue that it is better to form habits of complying with the laws of fair play and better for your neighbor not to form habits of leaning on others. So you may shake your head, "No." Of course, if he is having trouble with the subject, you may still be able to help him *afterward*, so that he develops his own understanding and ability and feels no need to cheat on an examination another time. That is having real respect for his identity and individuality, and is in line with Jewish tradition.

Now this explains how good and evil may operate within each person, affecting his own self. But it also shows how what he decides will affect other people; and we see at once how a person who has reached a position of great power would be able to, of his own choosing, bring enormous evil, or enormous good, into the lives of others.

"Job's Despair." Job is the prototype of human suffering, not denying God, but in anguish crying "Why"? This photograph is of a watercolor appearing in William Blake's Illustrations for the Book of Job.

Protest against suffering

From this comes the haunting question, why should the innocent be made to suffer through the evil deeds of others? And why should there be such enormous, such profound suffering at all in the world of man?

This "why" is the great outcry of man, and again it is best to realize at the outset that the answer is beyond our grasp. Glimmers have come to us. Every religion looks to God through this tormenting enigma.

Some religions declare that peace of soul comes through total acceptance and resignation. Judaism shows us that man may protest even to God Himself, but cautions us not to blaspheme and not to despair.

The first reaction to great suffering may be, "There is no God." Particularly when one sees pointless suffering, the pain of the infant stricken with a disease, the havoc of an earthquake, there may come a cry of rage and an urge toward atheism. The Talmud tells of Rabbi Elisha ben Avuyah who lost his faith when he saw a child fall from a tree and die. The child's father had asked the boy to get some eggs from a nest, and the Torah itself, the Rabbi knew, tells us it is permissible to take the eggs. The boy had done so, careful to perform the commandment of not taking the mother bird with the eggs. The Torah promises rewards to someone who obeys this commandment; but though he had done good, he lost his life. Where was the sin? What could possibly be the reason?

We know the cry of Job at the height of his suffering, both at the hands of nature and of man. He cursed the day of his birth and wanted to die. He protested to God. Yet in the end this parable shows Job regaining his humility before the mystery and vastness of God, as revealed in His creation.

One is reminded of Byron's hero, in *The Prisoner of Chillon*. This captive looked out upon the sea and mountains until, in the words of Lord Kenneth Clark, he "identified himself with the great forces of nature, and therefore with the sublime."

Names and dates, names and dates—a portion of the mourning scroll in Prague memorializing Czechoslovak Jews murdered in Nazi concentration camps.

In his awe before the Creator behind creation, Job reached the heights of sublimity where he could even—at God's direction—pray for his friends (Job's "comforters") who had so relentlessly raised false accusations against him in his illness and grief and loss. And we read in the epilogue to this drama that God changed the fortunes of Job when he prayed for his friends.

The problem of free will

The story of Job does not resolve the problem of evil. But it issues sharp warning—in God's rebuke to the three friends—against those who would superficially impute man's misfortunes to some alleged sin or sins. The story tells us that God's will is beyond man's comprehension, but it does not explain our suffering. For if God is merciful and compassionate, as we repeat so often in our praise of Him, why does He create such suffering? One reply that our philosophers give us is that man usually creates his own suffering, out of free will and bad choice. God does not create wars; this is man's work.

Then if God does not create war, we ask, why does He permit it?

Because God has given us free will, and if He interfered when man uses it badly, the whole process would be a mockery.

We may accept this as a partial answer but we keep on asking. Why, then, do we suffer from natural causes, from disease and from earthquakes and floods? How can a compassionate God inflict this on the innocent? We can find all sorts of speculations in the Talmud and in the reasoning of our thinkers; none are complete answers but they help us follow the moral growth of Judaism, they show us the human mind and soul in the very process of contending with God and achieving possession of one more spark of truth.

One rather curious suggestion is in the story we have read of the sinful Rabbi who prayed to the mountains and valleys only to be told that they too had sinned. Does this mean that a mountain can have "sinned" by the fall of rocks, causing death? Or just by being there? Sometimes we have such a notion of an evil element in the forces of nature itself. Not long ago a party of young people climbed on a pilgrimage to the top of Masada, where the last Judean heroes withstood the Romans. On their way down, a rockslide crushed two of the group. Was this evil on the part of the mountain? Curious vestiges of such beliefs remain in us. We still have feelings as though the forces of nature were being employed by God to carry out punishments.

This idea appears very early in the Bible, with the story of the flood. Noah accepts it, especially as he is to be exempt from the punishment. Later on the same idea appears when God tells Abraham that He is going to destroy Sodom and Gomorrah. But Abraham has made a covenant, he is the first Jew, and he protests to God. He pleads with God to save the city for the sake of fifty, even of ten, righteous men.

Challenging God

Here we see Judaism at its earliest point, expressing two ideas that are important to us. First, that nature may be used to punish evil, but secondly that we can challenge even God on moral grounds. Abraham bows to the idea of nature being used for destruction, but his demand for morality and justice remains.

It is when we cannot accept the idea of unjust punishment in our compassionate God that we search most desperately for another explanation that does not conflict with belief in Him. Thus we come to the concept of God whose spark is instilled in imperfect man. The totality of God may, or may not, be aware of each instant of each man. The moral action may rest within the God-spark in man himself. Mankind as a whole may fail to respond to this spark of conscience; so an Auschwitz can happen.

No theory will give us a final answer. But theories help us in thinking about this question. From our earliest teachings we may see good and evil as opposite ends of one idea. Just as we can think of darkness as an absence of light, the Talmud tells us, so we can think of evil as an absence of good.

A next step is to follow cause and effect. We can point to many good things that would not have happened but for something bad that preceded them. We are all in the habit of finding such connections in our daily life. Here is a young girl's romantic story: "If I hadn't put on high heels when my mother said not to, I wouldn't have been punished by tripping on the stairs and spraining my ankle. But if I hadn't tripped on the stairs I would never have met Harry, who came along just then and helped me. And now he is my boy friend."

We can follow that line of explanation to far greater events. For example, there is the theory that man's great medical discoveries are the balance of good for the existence of disease.

Problems of good and evil

How do we know the intention of God, the sages ask? What seems evil today may prove a blessing tomorrow, or in the final balance of existence. Yet the idea that what seems to us at first to be evil may really lead to good has already been turned away by the prophet Isaiah. "Woe unto them that say of evil, it is good, and of good, it is evil," he declared, crying out against those that "change darkness into light and light into darkness; that change bitter into sweet and sweet into bitter."

For this idea can make people seek evil with the excuse that it ends up in good. It can also lead to an overemphasis on martyrdom: it leads to the concept that the greatest sign of the love of God is in His greatest punishment, and causes some persons to seek such punishment. That is masochism.

Though Judaism instills admiration for genuine meekness, as in Moses, it does not idealize suffering, it does not idealize false humility, and it does not idealize the wicked.

The conviction that God does not want man to suffer spurs his efforts to find a cure for the "incurable." This research scientist is engaged in medical research.

If we follow the idea that the greatest good is through the greatest evil, we come to the extreme of debasement and debauchery, as was practiced by some of the false messiahs, claiming that the uttermost depths had to be reached before the world could be cleansed. The same thought is present among the dark sinners of a Dostoevski, pictured as reaching spirituality only through their sins.

Masochism appears in tales of monks, and saintly persons who flaggelate themselves, walk with sharp stones in their shoes, and practice other forms of self-punishment and torture in order to become pure. Such ideas have at times crept into the stream of Judaism, which is broad, but they have never constituted part of its character. Jews do not believe that God "wants man to suffer"—or to sin.

Even in the face of the Roman evil, the Rabbis did not counsel the Jews to seek martyrdom by openly defying Roman laws against Jewish worship. They taught that death is related to evil rather than to goodness. Our Passover folksong, *Had Gadya*, concludes with Eternity dissolving away Death itself.

But as Judaism examines both sides of every question, we must remember that we also revere the martyrs of Masada, among whom were religious zealots who chose mass suicide rather than submit Jewish families to the mockeries of the Romans.

Throughout history Jews have died for *kiddush ha-Shem*, the sanctification of the Name, the term for Jewish martyrdom.

God a spiritual force

It sometimes seems that evil need not have been put there in the first place. Thus a child may ask, why did God make polio? If it was only so that scientists could one day discover how to prevent the disease, why did it have to be there in the first place?

To this we may answer with the understanding that God, as in the story of creation, is a spiritual force—in Hebrew, the word *spirit* and the word for wind are the same, *ruah*; a moving force, or "everything that makes for the good," with chaos as the original material it works upon. The imperfect world, with its natural catastrophes, its diseases, and with imperfect man, all are in the process of being perfected out of chaos. Here again a modern view in Judaism links up with a "primitive" view in the Biblical story of creation. A wind, a spirit, a *ruah*, is at work upon chaos.

Even though Judaism has explored many explanations for suffering, including the idea that God is not aware of man, the tendency in Judaism is to feel God as a total awareness, a total compassion. We also feel that God is somehow accessible. We may contend with God; we feel truth in the epic story of Job, who demands that God explain the curses visited on a decent and worshipful man.

The story itself may today have distasteful aspects to us because it pictures a God who will torture a man simply on a wager with the Devil to test a man's faith. And because, in the end, Job reacts to a display of authoritative power. "Can you make the thunder?" he is asked, and that intimidates him. Noble as are many of the utterances in the Book of Job, we are nevertheless still left with the feeling that the story begs the question of suffering.

A "time of face-hiding"

In our time we have witnessed an evil so vast as to dwarf the example of Job. This was the holocaust, in which for over five years the Nazis, who were after all part of God's world, systematically tormented and murdered the Jews of Europe, so that scarcely half survived, and in some lands, scarcely a tenth. In all human history there is no single record of a planned evil so vast. The holocaust made atheists of many, it made still others adopt the explanation of a God who could not intervene, it made still others return to unquestioning faith in a last hope for the betterment of man.

Since Jews were the principal victims, what has this done for Judaism? As Jews are the conduit for the great moral stream of Biblical revelation, it seemed again as though, through this stunning happening to the Jews, some moral lesson was being offered to mankind. This enormous slaughter came upon a people who had a long experience of slaughter and they turned with it to an even more intensive examination, and seeking, for the meaning of God. Documents bearing testimony to this seeking were found among the ruins of the Warsaw ghetto, documents left by faithful Jews who perished in its destruction. Inspired by their accounts, and by the experiences they reflected, the writer Zvi Kolitz created the testimony of a modern Job, written in the midst of the flames that consumed him. His name was Yossel Rakover, and Zvi Kolitz recounts in *Yossel Rakover's Appeal to God* that on April 28, 1943, as fire from the German flame throwers in the rubble of the Warsaw ghetto reached him, he sat writing his last thoughts; that he hid them in a small bottle which was later found in the ruins.

I, Yossel, son of David Rakover of Tarnopol, a Chasid of the Rabbi of Ger, am writing these lines as the ghetto of Warsaw goes up in flames. The house in which I am at this moment is one of the last, which the flames have not yet reached. Now my hour has come, and like Job I could say of myself—and I am not the only one who can say this—naked did I come out of my mother's womb and naked will I return there. I am forty-three years old and as I look back over my life I can safely declare, inasmuch as a man can be certain about himself, that I led a righteous life. Once I was successful but I never allowed success to carry me away. My house was open to everyone in need, and I was happy whenever I could perform a good deed for my fellow men. I served my God fervently and my only desire of Him was that He grant me the fervor to serve Him, as it is written, "with all thy heart, with all thy soul, and with thy whole being." I cannot say, after all that has happened to me, that my feelings for God have not changed, but what I can say with all firmness is that my faith has not changed a bit. Formerly, as things were going well with me, my feelings for Him were as to one who showers goodness upon me, so that I also owed something to Him. Now my feelings to Him are as to one who owes me something. But I do not say, as did Job, "Tell me why Thou contendest with me?" Greater and better men than I are

Helpless Jews of the Warsaw ghetto, including dismayed mothers and wondering children, were rounded up by Nazi soldiers and sent off to their death in concentration camps.

now certain that it is not a question of crime and punishment, but that something very particular is happening on earth. This is a time of face-hiding.

God has hidden His face from His world and thereby has sacrificed His creatures to evil instincts. Therefore I believe, to my great regret, that it is almost natural that during a time when evil instincts rule in the world, the first victims are those in whom a divine spark lives, the pure ones. The believer has to see in these events a part of the great reckonings of God, in comparison with which the importance of the human tragedy is small. This does not mean that the believing Jew must justify this reckoning and say, God is just and His trial is just. To say that these punishments are due us would mean self-defamation and desecration of the Name.

There Yossel broke off, for the fire had reached him. But his last words are the essence of Judaism: even God can be called to judgment.

Yossel Rakover's words, "this is a time of face-hiding" are echoed by profound religious thinkers such as Martin Buber. The conception may be of a God who "hides His face" in anguish over the brutality of man, over horror at man's misuse of free will. Yet the believing man must call, must demand the presence of the face of God.

This image is anthropomorphic, for no matter how abstract our thinking about God, we are limited within ourselves. But this image of the absence of God really comes from its opposite, from the Jewish experience that has at times felt God to be present, very close to us and within us. And this searching for an explanation for suffering is a search to unite our experience of the world with our imperfect intuition of God.

To recapture God's presence

The words of Yossel Rakover were those of a man in the face of death. Out of the holocaust came a small proportion of survivors, among them a gifted writer named Elie Wiesel; he too insists that we must demand the "return" of God, that we must by our very fervor recapture His presence.

Wiesel, like Buber, is close to the Ḥasidic fervor, but even Martin Buber was shaken so deeply that he asked, "Can we still, as individuals and as a people, speak of God after the holocaust?"

Buber turns to a view of God as an "absolute personality," and clings to the idea, perhaps the wish, that even the absolute is approachable.

It is hard, very hard, to bring together our humanly limited idea of God with the experience of Auschwitz. Those who explain with the metaphor of the hidden face of God, remind us that the face of God has shone on so much that is good in human life. They remind us that most of us do not experience horror and grief except fleetingly and that the greatest part of life is blessed. Shall we say that the good things, as well as the bad, are bereft of God? Or shall we say that with the impulse from God, man has in some measure succeeded in conquering evil, and that even suffering from chaos in nature is slowly being abated by the control of these forces, learned by man, through the genius implanted in him by God?

These are some of the thoughts Judaism has used in seeking an answer to the question of suffering.

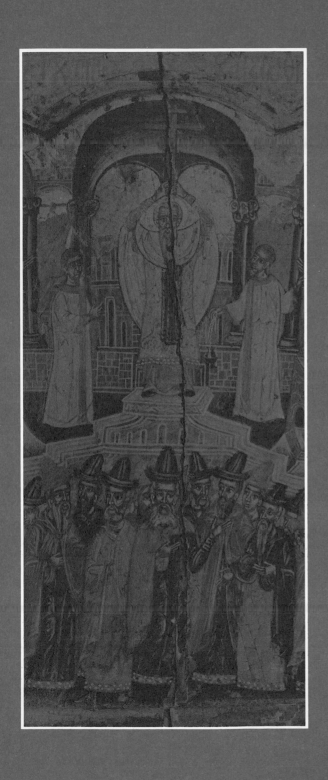

How shall we live with others in the world?

12 Jews with differing views

In Israel, a mother from a suburb of Tel Aviv told her friends a story about a visit with her six-year-old boy to the Orthodox neighborhood of Jerusalem, called Meah Shearim. When they got home the boy heard his parents talking about being Jewish. "But we are not Jewish!" he declared. "Why do you say that?" they asked. "Because we're not like *them*!" "Like who?" "Those men we saw today with the long coats and beards —*they* are Jewish!"

And Jews from New York's fine suburbs sometimes go, out of curiosity, to visit a section of Brooklyn called Williamsburg, where the same long coats and beards and side curls may be seen, and coming home they debate, "What do we have in common with those people?"

Some "modern" Jews are made uncomfortable because "those Jews" look so outlandish to them. Yet when they see the same type of "outlandish" Jew in East European clothing on the stage in *Fiddler on the Roof*, they sigh with nostalgic love and pride. For they then see the "old-fashioned" Jew in his historic setting of time and place, where his appearance is natural and not "outlandish." And they think, "Those were the real Jews."

A search for identity

There is a noted short story called "Eli the Fanatic," by a modern American Jewish writer, Philip Roth, about a young husband in a middle-class suburb. As it happens, a group of survivors from the holocaust, all wearing Ḥasidic garb, open a *yeshivah* in a mansion in this town. The middle-class Jews are upset to see those Jews with round hats and long black coats walking about their shopping district. Finally Eli donates a suit of clothes to the head of the *yeshivah* for the use of the teacher who most frequently comes into town. Shortly thereafter he is startled when the Ḥasid in return leaves a suit of Ḥasidic clothing for *him.* In his confusion over the meaning of Jewish identity, the sophisticated Eli dons the Ḥasidic garb and goes out into the town. Eventually all this brings him to a nervous breakdown and the need for psychiatric treatment.

Things are really not that bad. Although the extremes in Jewish views may be far apart in outward appearance, Judaism does have an inner unity. Indeed from the very first, the tradition of Judaism is filled with argument and dissent, and this has proved healthy. This shows that the people care, and care very much, even fanatically, about their faith. As long as people debate their ideas, beliefs, and the practice of their religion, it remains alive and meaningful.

The Meah Shearim section of Jerusalem. The man in Ḥasidic garb and the buildings with overhung second story suggest the quiet ways of an earlier day.

Historic divisions in Judaism

From the very beginning there was the basic argument about "old" and "new," between Orthodoxy and Reform, between dutiful worship and meaningful worship, between Jews remaining a closed society, and what we now call acculturation.

From the time of King David there was the struggle between the priests, who carried out the exact rules of the sacrifices on the altar, and the prophets, who said God does not care about your incense and burning flesh, He cares for justice.

The answer of the strictly observant, to such reformers, has always been, "We care for justice too, as much and perhaps more than you do, but we also perform the rites as a constant reminder, and as a discipline."

In the days of the Second Temple there was a profound struggle between the Sadducees and the Pharisees. And for centuries there was a struggle between the Karaites, a rather fanatic sect, who said they would go only by the exact rules of the Five Books of Moses, and the Rabbis who made interpretations of those rules and interpretations of the interpretations. Descendants of the Karaites are still to be found today, though the sect is deemed broken off from Judaism.

Though not unlimited in elasticity, Judaism spreads over many divided interpretations through the unity of belief in the ethical purpose of life. Yet many Jews have little understanding of the differences within that unity.

Orthodox, Reform, and Conservative groups

In the United States, where the largest number of Jews live, there are three different groups of synagogues, in the main: the Orthodox, Reform, and Conservative. They are roughly equal in numbers. In Israel, Orthodox worship is somewhat of an official religion, so there are few other congregations, and in other countries the proportions vary.

The variations in Jewish services are explained by Rabbi Eugene Borowitz on a philosophical basis. "The central idea in the difference is whether traditional Jewish law is basically God's creation, or man's response to God."

If God really created each law, then man cannot change it by a single point. Thus, the Orthodox insist, man can only interpret God's law.

If the law is man's response to God, then he is free to work on and change his response, according to his own development over the years and centuries. This freedom, one extremely "advanced" rabbi insisted, nearly a century ago, can go all the way to a rejection of circumcision. After all, it can be argued anthropologically that this is simply a tribal rite. Yet as a symbol of the covenant it is deeply imbedded in the Jewish psyche; as may be expected, there were few followers of this proposal, and it was dropped. It is a rare extreme of this sort that shocks Orthodox Jews into declaring that Reform followers are hardly Jews at all.

The Reform, on the other hand, reply that they represent what is most alive in Judaism, which otherwise could become stultified. Far from neglecting Jewish scholarship and tradition, they study it deeply.

The Conservative view, as the name declares, is less ready to accept changes, particularly where they appear to arise from acculturation rather than from an inner need in Judaism itself. They feel themselves equally with the Reform movement in the progress of Judaism.

Each section in Judaism has its own training centers for rabbis; every Reform candidate has to acquire a knowledge of the Talmud and the commentaries, though not necessarily as studied in the Orthodox academies or *yeshivot*. In addition, the Conservative and Reform candidates may have a wider program in the social sciences. Indeed, the American Reform candidates now even have a special branch in Jerusalem for the study of archaeology.

But we must not imagine that Orthodoxy is petrified. Professor Salo Baron reminds us that Polish Jewry, in the year just before the Nazis began their destruction, produced a formidable number of books in such fields as Law, Aggadah, Kabbalah, and Ḥasidism, more studies in one year than in any twenty years of the height of Rabbinic learning two centuries ago.

But books alone do not measure religious faith. The Orthodox argue that the Reform and even the Conservative Jew does not really feel religious and that he is on the way to assimilation. The Reform Jew retorts that the prayers of the Orthodox Jew are by rote, that they are mere lip service, and that it is the moral practice of Judaism in every act of life that counts.

A range of interpretations

One of the most oft-repeated prayers in all branches of the Jewish faith can be interpreted both ways. It follows the Shema. Many stories say that the Shema alone, *Hear O Israel: the Lord our God, the Lord is One,* is enough to save the soul of a Jew if he has strayed far afield and can remember no more.

After the Shema, tradition tells us to say:

And thou shalt love the Lord thy God with all thy heart, with all thy soul, and with all thy might. And these words which I command thee this day shall be upon thy heart: thou shalt teach them diligently unto thy children, and shalt speak of them when thou sittest in thy house, when thou walkest by the way, when thou liest down, and when thou risest up. And thou shalt bind them for a sign upon thy hand, and they shall be for frontlets between thine eyes. And thou shalt write them upon the doorposts of thy house, and upon thy gates.

We are told of a pious man who took this instruction from Moses so literally that he would lie down when he repeated the words "when thou liest down." And we remember the story of the good Jew who was punished for the "sin" of putting his "frontlet between the eyes" before he wound the *Tefillin* on his arm.

Yet this same prayer, which led to *Mezuzot* on our doorposts, may be, in modern terms, quite simply interpreted as meaning we should always, in waking, in going on our way, in going to bed, keep in mind the ethical meaning of Judaism, and be careful to teach this to our children.

The Reform Jew feels this is expressed in the quotation from the prophet Micah, "What doth the Lord require of thee but to do justly, and love mercy, and walk humbly with thy God?"

What more does the Lord ask? To the Orthodox the Lord asks a sign of devotion, or obedience, in every act of life. And the neo-Orthodox, or new Orthodox, including some modern intellectuals, tell us that such devotion is more than mere superstition and taboo. It is a discipline, a heightening of prosaic existence, a wish to express reverence in each gesture of daily life, in the way food is prepared, in the blessing over bread and wine, in greeting people, in touching the *Mezuzah*. It is, as in art, a control of life, but with a constant reminder in repeating the phrase, "If such be the will of God."

Jewish practices and customs

Those may be the ways of extreme persons, we say, but how does the difference between Orthodox, Conservative, and Reform show itself among "ordinary" Jews?

We know, of course, the basic signs of difference in the synagogue: The Orthodox keeps his head covered, and the men sit apart from the women; there is no instrumental music, only the voice; the prayers are long and sometimes without decorum.

In the Conservative synagogue the Jew keeps his head covered but the women usually sit with the men, and there is an atmosphere of decorum. Customs differ as to music.

In the Reform synagogue the head is generally uncovered, the women sit with the men, there may be organ music, with a choir.

There is also a considerable difference in worship. The pious Orthodox Jew prays on rising, either at home or in the synagogue, putting on *Tefillin* and *Tallit*. If at home, the morning prayers may take only fifteen or twenty minutes; if he goes to the *shul*, he may take part in a full service, with the Torah brought out and the portion read. Then he may sit down with the others for a while, in the custom of studying a page from the Talmud. The leader will read and everyone may join in discussing the commentaries. All of this will take a good hour or more.

A number of Conservative synagogues also conduct this full morning prayer service, the *Shaḥarit*, while most Reform synagogues do not.

In the late afternoon, the Orthodox Jew will again, either at home or in his synagogue, repeat the given prayers, the *Minḥah*, shorter now, about ten minutes. And in the evening—*Arvit*. The first two of these services are based on the ordained sacrifices of the Temple, continuing in the synagogue and at home what was destroyed in Jerusalem. The observant Jew, Orthodox, Conservative, or Reform will of course attend Sabbath services both on the eve and during the day, and perform the *Havdalah* at the close of the Sabbath. After the services on the eve of Sabbath, or again on the Sabbath afternoon, an informal gathering called *Oneg Shabbat*—the pleasure of Sabbath—is held, with discussions, singing, and refreshments.

The Conservative and Reform synagogues usually emphasize community activities more than do the Orthodox. There may be everything from a political meeting to a course in Bible archaeology or even on the Talmud. There will be lectures on modern Jewish literature, art exhibits, theatricals. Fund-raising meetings for Israel and for local causes are, of course, common. Civil rights causes and educational problems are in the foreground. The Conservative movement as well as the Reform are, more often than the Orthodox, directed to the whole social and community life of the Jew, including his contact with a non-Jewish environment.

Often the borders between the three movements are hard to define. Much depends on the individual rabbi. In Israel, where the Reform movement is just beginning, some rabbis have chosen to keep the custom of the covered head, rather than the bare head. But still the Board of Rabbis in Jerusalem, which is entirely Orthodox, will not admit a Reform or Conservative rabbi into their authority, and will not allow such rabbis to perform valid marriages.

Although there are many differences in details, and although the Orthodox, Conservative, and Reform in the United States each have their own rabbinical association, the three groups have been joined since 1926 in a joint rabbinic and lay organization, the Synagogue Council of America.

Ḥasidim and Mitnagdim

Recently, with the spread of interest in Judaism, we have learned more about earlier differences between Jewish religious groups, such as the *Ḥasidim* and *Mitnagdim* in Poland and Russia. We think of the present-day *Ḥasidim* as extremely punctilious in their worship. In their early days they were accused of being ignorant and almost pagan. They were a grassroots movement, and Ḥasidism became enormously popular. The more established rabbis, highly opposed to the "wonder-workers," were simply called "The Opponents" or *Mitnagdim*. The Jews in what was then the great heartland of Judaism became so violently divided between Ḥasidim and Mitnagdim that the two groups would scarcely allow their sons and daughters to intermarry. We have a modern American novel about a boy from a Ḥasidic family and a boy from a regular Orthodox family in Brooklyn, which tells how they became great friends after an intense rivalry between their two schools in a baseball game. The popularity of this novel, *The Chosen*, by Chaim Potok, indicates to us the serious and lively interest in Judaism in our land today.

The Reconstructionists

One more form of Judaism, one that has arisen in America, is an offshoot of the Conservative movement, has a small number of synagogues of its own, but claims rabbis in both the Conservative and Reform groups. They call themselves "Reconstructionists," after the philosophy of Rabbi Mordecai Kaplan. Rabbi Kaplan called for a "reconstruction" of Jewish life, seeing Judaism as a whole, as a "civilization."

In this, religion is the central force, but far from the only force. Jewish life is also ethnic, it is related to Israel, it has legal, linguistic, literary, and artistic expression. The American Jew then shares in two civilizations, the American and the Jewish, with the cultural life of Israel as part of the Jewish component. This is complex, but so is our place in society. To try too much to simplify our lives, to insist on making life all of one piece, can lead to prejudice, rigidity, and sometimes amputation.

Rabbi Kaplan teaches a Judaism that flows freely with the current of life. He sees danger in indifference, in turning away when Judaism seems to have no immediate bearing on an "outside" situation. A broader view of Judaism will show there is a relationship, and will help us partake in social actions not only with a view of "what is good for the Jews" but what is good for humanity.

Unity in diversity

Thus the range of worship within Judaism is wide and adaptable. Yet all groups turn to the same basic prayers, the same holidays, the same Bible, and unite with the same past. All try to live the same ethical life. Unity far outweighs outward differences.

As the famed Gaon of Vilna, the renowned Talmudic scholar Elijah was leader of the Mitnagdim, stern opponents of the Ḥasidim.

13 Israel, America

Deciding what kind of Jew you are when it comes to religious observance is one of the living aspects of Judaism. Judaism requires you to make decisions, to participate in the unending discussion and discovery that began with Abraham. Indeed you may, during your life, go from one style of worship to another, and back to the first.

Jewish loyalties

Such flexibility in Judaism also applies to another question that each person must answer for himself—that of a Jew's relationship to Israel, though he is a citizen of another nation.

Your grandfathers, before the State of Israel was reborn, might well have declared, "I would only be too happy to have such a problem!" Indeed this particular question, in a formal way, has not existed for Jews from the time the Romans destroyed Jerusalem until the present era.

In an informal way, the Jewish community, wherever it lived, under whatever government, was always asking itself, about each governmental decision, "Is this good or bad for the Jews?" But from the end of the Bar Kokhba revolt against the Romans, until 1948 when Israel again became a nation in Judea, Jews living elsewhere did not have to face in its full political sense the question that has been raised as "dual loyalty."

This same question had been faced in the past, centuries before the Roman occupation. It was raised when the Jews were first driven out of their land and taken to Babylonia. When, half a century later, they were permitted to return home, a large proportion remained settled in Babylonia, and remained Jewish. The problem was raised for them only partially, since Babylonia and Judea had both become parts of the Persian empire of Darius. Still, it was raised in one way or another in every ancient city where a Jewish community flourished. Even while Jerusalem stood, there were Jewish tribes in Arabia, there were Jewish settlements in Mesopotamia, in Greece, and Egypt, and Rome. Under Greek, and then Roman, rule the Jewish community in Alexandria grew to over a million, and a large Jewish population remained in that city under Egyptian rule until very recent times. Jews were the loyal subjects of the rulers of those lands, for the answer to this question had been given from the outset, in Babylon, by the Rabbis, and was written into the Talmud: "The law of the land where you reside is your law."

This was the rule for the civil laws and for national allegiance. But the Jewish communities within themselves dealt with religious laws and with all matters left to them by the local governments. For their religious rulings they looked to their sages.

Division in the Diaspora

After Jerusalem was destroyed, the Jews spread farther and farther into lands that were to become Germany and Poland and Russia and Spain and America. Though in many places there were special laws, and often special taxes, applied to them, Jews did their best as loyal subjects, and eventually as full citizens, wherever they lived. Sometimes, as in the First World War, they found themselves in opposing armies, fighting each other, French Jews against German Jews, for example. Each Jew was patriotic and proud of his nationality, though Jews could not help feeling more acutely than others the tragedy of national quarrels when all men are brothers.

The memory of such situations haunts us when we raise the question of "dual loyalty." Now that there is a Jewish nation, could not the time come when we, as citizens of another land, would have to oppose Israel? Or even, in the most horrible of suppositions, be called on to fight, or to support a fight, against fellow Jews in their own land?

Such an extreme possibility is unlikely to come for American Jews, but we should examine this idea if only to help ourselves understand basic questions of loyalty, patriotism, religion, and conflicting beliefs. We are not the first, or by any means alone, in facing such questions.

In the First and Second World Wars, American citizens of German origin faced a similar dilemma. In the First World War, they had to weigh their American loyalty and their faith in our democratic system against the call of the *Vaterland* and the aims of the Kaiser to enlarge Germanic power in the world and spread German *kultur*. There were indeed loyalty scares in America, spy scares, and internments, though generally German Americans chose democracy and fought in the Allied armies.

This dark time was repeated for German Americans in the Second World War, when the cause was even more clear, since Germany was a Fascist, antidemocratic power. Though the Nazis had organized followers among German Americans, the German American community as a whole was anti-Fascist and loyal to the Allied cause. Japanese Americans, called *Nisei,* had the same problem, and it was one of the shameful aspects of the war that on the West Coast Japanese Americans were interned in special camps out of distrust of their loyalty. Yet special units of Nisei volunteered and distinguished themselves in the Army. With them, as with the German Americans, what weighed most strongly was a fight for the democratic idea against the Fascist way of life. It was not only a question of national loyalty, or patriotism for patriotism's sake, that faced each such person, but also a question of war aims.

"Somewhere in the Middle East" Jewish soldiers from twenty-five nations march in the Jewish battalion formed within the British army to combat Nazism in World War II.

Conflicts of loyalties

The same might be said not only for people with a birth problem about loyalties, but about everyone in the world today. Loyalty to an idea is often in basic conflict with loyalty to a government. Over the war in Vietnam, many good Americans felt their very souls torn apart by such a conflict of loyalties. There is no way to escape conflict in life except by renouncing the very gift, painful though it can sometimes be, of being a man. And if being a Jew sometimes raises one more conflicting question, as in regard to Israel, we should look at it from the highest point of view. We should examine the principles that are involved in each problem as it arises, instead of following any automatic rule or any public fever.

In the event of war, it is possible that a nation will call on men who have ties on the other side. Israel itself has already gone through this experience again and again with its own Arab citizenry. But let us not avoid the question by posing only its extreme aspect, the case of war. There are lesser conflicts that arise every day, such as, should Jews object to permitting anti-Israel propaganda in America? On each question each Jew must think out his own position.

Shared beliefs in democracy

Fortunately, in their basic outlook Israel and the United States are much alike. Both stand for progress through democracy. American Jews do not find themselves in the dreadful position of Russian Jews who know that the national policy is anti-Israel, and who dare not express the slightest sympathy for their own people in that land, even in religious terms.

The shared belief in democracy helps us and lessens the danger of total conflict. But in the complicated game of world politics, with oil interests, world trade, security, and rivalry for power, it is always possible that this kinship in ideals will not be enough to keep America and Israel on the same side. How should the American Jew think about himself, if this happens? It is a serious question since most Jews feel an historical, mythic, and spiritual link with Israel.

Arguments of the American Council for Judaism

Strangely enough, some Jews who are anti-Israel make their argument out of this religious bond. They say we are Jews by religion alone, and we have no special ties to a secular nation of Jews living in Palestine, a large part of whom are even non-religious! Such views come from a group few in number but quite wealthy, and therefore able to put out a great deal of propaganda. They call themselves the American Council for Judaism. They seem to be terrified by this question of "dual loyalty."

The oversimple argument of this Council, and of others who share their fear, appears logical. But it is exactly because life is not that simple, exactly because our Jewish situation is really a special one, that we are valuable to the world. No matter what comparisons are drawn, no matter what parallels are seen—to the Irish-Americans, to the Armenians, to other religious groups, to other ethnic groups, as the Negroes, there always remains some part that doesn't fit. The Jews are the foremost reminder to mankind of the individuality of every people and of every person.

Judaism versus chauvinism

The Jewish quality, the Jewish situation in many lands, is a damper on the brutal kind of nationalism called *chauvinism.* The Jewish presence raises questions of "right" as against the blind loyalty of "my country right or wrong."

Israel, for example, is generally accused of being "highly nationalistic"—because it fights for its national life. Yet Israel is composed of Jews from all nations, each of whom has at least a family remembrance, often a geographical sentiment, for some other land. All this leads to a consideration of many points of view, and to a highly cosmopolitan people rather than to a narrow nationalism.

In the same way, Jews living in other countries, loyal citizens of those countries, yet feeling a profound historical connection to Jerusalem, are less likely to hold narrow chauvinistic views wherever they live. We readily see this at any moment in any country in the world. Jews are in the forefront of those who raise questions of social justice in South Africa, in South America, in North America. It is the peculiar position of the Jew to be such a witness in the world; it is the entwinement of loyalties in his soul that makes him sensitive to all issues. We should not be afraid of this. We should use it; the combined vision of two eyes gives us our sense of depth.

The extreme views of the assimilated,

Under the supervision of the Israeli Pioneer Corps (Nahal) is this cow farm—not in Israel but on the Ivory Coast. Jewish teaching calls for loving our neighbor and for showing that love in practical ways.

well-to-do Jews who guide the American Council for Judaism, and of some of their followers, are what most of us would call devices to avoid the task of really working out our own relationship to Israel.

Emigration to Israel

Let us take another extreme, the Jew who feels a total passion for Israel, whose thoughts are entirely on what goes on there, who has little or no interest in American activities or problems. Why, then, perhaps such a person should try to arrange his life so as to become an Israeli citizen. That is a clean answer, and a small steady number of American Jews, from the very beginning of the Zionist movement, have taken this course. To change one's nationality is hardly rare in this world. America itself was established by people who chose to do so.

Among Americans who adopted this path in Zionism, the first that comes to mind is, of course, Golda Meir. She was born in Russia, raised in Milwaukee, went to Palestine shortly after the Balfour Declaration, and eventually became Prime Minister of Israel. From Canada there was Dov Joseph, who joined the Jewish Brigade in the First World War and eventually became Minister of Justice in Israel. In the thirties, small groups of American pioneers founded such kibbutzim as Ein ha-Shofet and K'far Blum. And after the Second World War, numbers of Americans volunteered to man illegal immigrant ships, and still more went to fight for Israel's independence. Some of these became Israelis. Others discovered they still felt American and, their task done, like volunteers for any cause, they came home and settled back into their American Jewish lives.

Meanwhile young Jews of a newer generation, not in vast numbers, but each out of careful consideration and self-examination, decided to make their lives in Israel. To most, it was an intense experience providing the sense of "doing something with their lives" as against prosaic middle-class existence in America. New kibbutzim, such as Sasa, were founded, and so were various factories and enterprises. A constantly growing flow of scholars settled to teach at the Hebrew University; indeed, the university's first president was an American—Judah Magnes. Other American Jewish scientists have joined Bar Ilan, the Tel Aviv, Haifa, and Beersheba universities, the American College in Jerusalem, and the Weizmann Institute—founded by an American, Meyer Weisgal. Such is the case when the American Jew wants a total identification as a Jew, or finds a creative, absorbing work in Israel.

Visitors to Israel

By far the greatest number of American Jews who go to Israel, however, aside from the thousands of tourists, are those who go for a few months or a year to study or simply to live there. The Hebrew University and the universities of Bar Ilan and of Tel Aviv each year receive thousands of students from abroad, mostly from America.

It has long been a goal for American students to live in Europe for a year, so as to make contact with an older civilization. For the Jew going to Israel, the contact is obviously deeper. The proportion of students who decide to remain and make their lives in Israel is not great; the enrichment of their Israeli studies is carried home to America. Such young people give us our best understanding of the complex question of loyalties. Usually the drastic quality of the question dissolves away. They have gone close enough really to know what is American in them and what touches Israel, and to be able to judge each problem on merit as it arises.

A clear example of the way in which a Jew faces this whole question is that of Arthur Goldberg, who, as the American Ambassador to the United Nations (1965–1968), spoke for the American political position even when he had at times to condemn Israel. Yet Arthur Goldberg belonged to a Zionist club in his college days, and is a leader in many American Jewish organizations that help Israel. The central line of his life remains in American public affairs.

Arthur J. Goldberg addressing the General Assembly of the United Nations in New York.

Nationalism and moral values

The problem of national loyalty, whether it faces the Jew, the Negro, or the American of Japanese, German, or Irish descent, is a problem that opens up to us the whole question of the place and mission of man in the world. Nationalism is a powerful cause in moving men to war. When we want to arouse people to this cause we call it patriotism. But when we see nationalism as blind and destructive, in the way it was used by the Nazis, we must also fear it as a force.

Political leaders can play with the emotions of a people, and by calling on their patriotism drive them into a dictatorship, or into wars of aggression, as well as defense. Each man in the end must try to be his own judge, even of his own nation, his own people. More and more people believe that the national impulse must be constantly examined. The peace of all the nations of the world is of the greatest importance. An individual who, in his life, has had to decide in a crisis between two claims on his loyalty (citizenship and origin), between being a Japanese and being an American, as in the Second World War, or being a German and an American, as in two world wars, is more likely to think about what each cause stands for than to fight out of blind hatred or blind allegiance. In this sense the Jew has had the greatest experience of all. He has lived in all the lands of the earth, and fought for every cause, and has measured them all with the profound moral teaching that is Judaism.

Joy and concern over Israel

It is not a nationalistic feeling that the Jew gets from Israel, but a sense of unity with time, with history, with God, and a moral sense of uplift in the courage and achievement of his people.

An American Jewish poet, Karl Shapiro, expressed this feeling in the very tones of an Isaiah:

When I think of the liberation of Palestine,
When my eye conceives the great black English
    line

Spanning the world news of two thousand years,
My heart leaps forward like a hungry dog,
My heart is thrown back on its tangled chain,
My soul is hangdog in a Western chair.

When I think of the battle for Zion I hear
The drop of chains, the starting forth of feet,
And I remain chained in a Western chair.
My blood beats like a bird against a wall,
I feel the weight of prisons in my skull
Falling away; my forebears stare through stone.

When I see the name of Israel high in print
The fences crumble in my flesh; I sink
Deep in a Western chair and rest my soul.
I look the stranger clear to the blue depths
Of his unclouded eye. I say my name
Aloud for the first time unconsciously.

Speak of the tillage of a million heads
No more. Speak of the evil myth no more
Of one who harried Jesus on his way
Saying, Go faster. Speak no more
Of the yellow badge, secta nefaria.
Speak the name only of the living land.

And Abraham Heschel said:

There is a cure of the soul in the concern on the part of the Jews everywhere for the people who live in the State of Israel. The State may be thousands of miles away, but the care we feel is intimate and strong. Such care may serve as an example to all mankind. To be concerned for the security and well-being of man everywhere is a concern that we must cultivate all the time, without qualification. Wherever a man is harmed, we are all hurt.

The way that leads out of the darkness is peace between brothers, care for our fellow man. To care for our brother ardently, actively, is a way of worshiping God, a way of loving God.

14 Jews, Jesus, and Christianity

Up to our time there were few Jewish homes in which a reasonable discussion about Jesus could take place. Even those Jews who read the New Testament did so as if they were reading something forbidden. Immigrant Jews from the *shtetl* were likely to walk a little faster or even to cross the street when passing a church. Your parents can probably tell you about being called "Christ killers" when they were little, or you may even have had this experience yourself.

But today it is more likely that you have been taken on an interfaith visit to a Christian church, and have been told that in the main conduct of life Jews and Christians pretty much believe the same way, in the Ten Commandments, the Golden Rule, in seeking peace, in helping the poor. Why, then, you may have wondered, did the good Christians in the past shed so much Jewish blood?

Important religious differences

America, you may have read, is really based on Judaeo-Christian civilization, that is, on the Old and New Testaments, for of course Christianity includes our own Bible in its teaching. You may also have read about ecumenism, in which different beliefs seek points in common. Since the Second World War, this movement has grown. It has had a wholesome effect against prejudice and intolerance, but to find points in common does not mean to have the same beliefs. Christians and Jews may agree about some of the teachings repeated by Jesus, but will never agree about his divinity.

It is necessary for the Jew, if he wants to understand himself, as well as his Christian neighbors, to know about Jesus and also to know about a quite different subject, the religion built in his name, Christianity. Instead of shuddering and turning away from the church, the Jew should respect the good it has done and can achieve, and the genuine religious emotion of Christians. He should also know the church's errors.

Life and teachings of Jesus

The story of Jesus is told in the New Testament in four parallel accounts, the earliest written about thirty years after his death. Three of these Gospels highly resemble each other, while the fourth adds some incidents and changes others. Each was written in a different center of early Christianity and tailored to the local needs. Modern scholars have tried to puzzle out what really happened by comparing the Gospels. Some events they describe, such as the birth of Jesus, have, through holidays like Christmas, become part of the American way of life.

We are told that Jesus, or Yehoshua, was born of Mary, the wife of Joseph, a carpenter of Nazareth, just after they had had to journey to Bethlehem, her home town, to register for the Roman census. Some scholars say this was really put in to prove that Jesus was descended from the family line of King David, linked to Bethlehem. In this way the story could fit the prophecy that Messiah would be descended from David.

The boy Yehoshua was raised in Nazareth, but at an early age, we read, astonished the teachers in Jerusalem with his grasp of the Torah. Until he was about thirty, we are told little else except that he was baptized by Johanan, or John, a prophet who declared that Messiah was about to appear, and who dipped his followers in the waters of the Jordan River, as a rite of purification. Later, in the Christian code, this rite of baptism was to become a substitute for circumcision.

Jesus began preaching in Galilee, healing, and performing miracles. He collected a group of twelve disciples and sent them out to heal and preach, and as "fishers of men" to collect followers. His own preaching, most often quoted from the Sermon on the Mount, has been shown by Professor Joseph Klausner and others to be drawn almost entirely from previous Jewish teachings. His sayings are beautifully put; he favors the poor, he reaffirms the Golden Rule to love thy neighbor as thyself, and he extends this teaching by saying "Love thine enemy." He seems gentle, and a pacifist, but at other times he is harsh, crying out, "I come not to bring peace but a sword." He scrupulously follows Jewish observance, declaring he would not change a jot or tittle of the Law,

The gentle side of Jesus was reflected by St. Francis of Assisi. A thirteenth-century French Psalter shows the saint preaching love to the birds.

but like Hillel he is compassionate and lenient. For example, when he judges a woman taken in adultery, it is not with punishment but simply by saying, "Go and sin no more." The most quoted example of his life attitude, which has a puzzling tone for the Jew, is his advice to "turn the other cheek" when slapped. This could be simple meekness, it could be moral strength, it could also be a form of passive resistance against the Romans. It has been used to teach restraint of violence in our nature.

Jesus is an inspired teller of parables, a favorite form of moral teaching used by Nathan and other prophets. He lets it be understood that he is the Messiah; he even raises the dead if people but believe in him. At the height of his popularity, Jesus and his followers make the traditional Passover pilgrimage to Jerusalem. He sends for a white donkey in order to fulfill the belief that Messiah shall enter Jerusalem on such an animal. In the Temple, he violently drives out the money-changers, who are there to change Roman coins, some of which had forbidden images on them, into shekels for buying sheep and doves for the sacrifice.

Betrayal and trial

At the Seder, held with his twelve closest disciples, Jesus predicts he will be betrayed. And in the Garden of Gethsemane, to which he goes with Peter and two disciples, Judas, one of the twelve, points him out to the authorities. Jesus is taken, we are told, to a special hearing before the High Priest, he is condemned as "worthy of death," but turned over to Pontius Pilate, the Roman governor, who sentences him as a rebel, and he is crucified under the sign, "King of the Jews."

In one account, the Gospel of St. Matthew, Pontius Pilate formally "washes his hands" of the whole affair. Pilate has offered to free Jesus or some other prisoner, in accordance with a Passover custom. (There is no historic knowledge of such a custom.) Instead of Jesus, the Jewish mob chooses Barabbas, described as a thief, for freedom. And Matthew's account here provides the slogan for centuries of persecution and slaughter of Jews, for he has the Jewish crowd insist on death for Jesus, crying out, "His blood is on us and our children forever."

Taken down from the cross, Jesus is placed in a burial cave, but three days later he is seen, risen from the dead. He shows himself several times to his disciples and others. Then he ascends to heaven.

Soon his closest followers establish a sect, declaring he was indeed the Messiah, and will return again. The head of this group is his brother James. All the members are good Jews who worship at the Temple. James is executed by the Romans, and another relative becomes the leader of this first church.

About thirty years later, in the year 70, when the Romans destroyed Jerusalem, this early church disappeared, but by then there were other churches in Alexandria, Rome, Corinth, and various cities of the Mediterranean area. However, a split had already taken place between the "circumcisers" and the "uncircumcisers," between those who wanted to keep the sect Jewish and those who preached to all who would listen. When the earlier church vanished in the destruction of Jerusalem, the church of the "uncircumcisers" developed into Christianity as we know it. But before exploring this, it is interesting to look at some of the recent scholarship about the life of Jesus, especially *Jesus and the Zealots*, by a highly respected authority, S. G. F. Brandon.

Background of Jesus' execution

One of the most puzzling points about the story of Jesus is the reason for his execution by the Romans. If he had been only a Jewish preacher, a popular healer who showed great pity for the poor and heavyladen, why should he be sentenced to crucifixion?

Professor Brandon and other scholars have become convinced that Jesus was involved with a secret resistance movement against the Romans. When we consider some of the resistance movements of our own time we can picture this more clearly. During the British control of Palestine, there were three such movements, the Haganah, the Irgun, and the Stern group, sometimes working together, sometimes violently against each other, while there were also Jews who wanted to collaborate with the British. In Roman times, it was the wealthy, aristocratic families from among whom the High Priests were chosen, who were the collaborators. The Romans permitted Jewish worship at the Temple, but had even taken over the appointment of the High Priest and the control of the holy vestments. The simple, pious members of the populace resented these highly placed collaborators.

Roman rule was severe, the tax burden was unbearable, and in the countryside resistance movements sprang up. Various messiahs appeared, performing wonders and miracles, and promising an end to the suffering of the people, promising the return of an independent Jewish kingdom. When Jesus was a boy of nine or ten in Nazareth, the most popular resistance leader was a man named Judah of Galilee, head of the Zealots. So strong was his movement that, at least according to the writings of Josephus, over half a century later it was a descendant of Judah of Galilee who commanded the last stand at Masada.

One of the Zealots is listed among the twelve disciples of Jesus—he is called Simon the Zealot. This not only shows that Jesus and the resistance fighters were acceptable to each other, but raises the question whether there was not what we would today call a common front. When Jesus "drove out the money-changers" he staged a revolt against the collaborators who operated the profitable Temple concessions. At the same time, Professor Brandon points out, there was an uprising in another part of Jerusalem, and Bar Abba [Barabbas] was among the leaders captured by the Romans. Though Jesus was crucified, we are popularly told, "between two thieves," these were actually two resistance leaders, for the Romans called such men "bandits" just as today freedom fighters are often called "bandits" by their opponents. Crucifixion was the Roman punishment for revolt, and Jesus was sentenced

by Pontius Pilate as a rebel, mockingly called "King of the Jews."

False condemnation of the Jews

What, then, did the Jews have to do with the death of Jesus? It seems clear that much of the populace was ready to believe in Jesus, who had overtly entered Jerusalem as the Messiah. In those days, this meant the God-sent leader who would free the Jews from Roman rule. The idea of a golden Messianic Age for all of mankind was to grow, later, and this enlargement of the messianic idea is indeed at first a Christian contribution. But to Jesus and the Jews of his time the freeing of the Temple from collaborators could well be seen as the beginning of messianic action. Over such an action, the Roman-appointed High Priest could find himself in trouble with the authorities. What was happening? Were the Jews trying to capture the Temple as a stronghold, in the beginning of their fight for freedom? If Jesus was apprehended and brought before the High Priest for questioning, it would be logical for that collaborator to denounce his claims as Messiah, and to turn him back to the civil authorities—the Romans. They sentenced him as a rebel.

Why then did the Christian Gospels put the blame for the death of Jesus entirely on the Jews, with one of the Gospels even inserting the dreadful scene of Jews crying out, "His blood is on us and our children forever!" The four Gospels were written from thirty to sixty years later, and none of them by people who witnessed the events. They were written for Christian groups under Roman rule in different cities such as Alexandria or Rome, groups that feared Roman persecution and therefore clearly did not want to invite trouble by accusing the Romans of killing their God! For by then, Jesus had been declared not only the Messiah, but the Son of God and a unity with God. The early Christians also knew that the Romans, having just finished a costly and bloody war with the Jews, were suspicious of a group that reverenced a Jew. What more simple than to put all the blame on the Jews, rather than the Romans, for the death of Jesus? Pontius Pilate "washing his hands" of the affair, and the Jews actually demanding to take the blame, forever! These lines were to produce pogroms and massacres of Jews down through the centuries. Only in very recent years, after anti-Semitism had resulted in the Nazi holocaust, was the Christian conscience shocked enough for the church to disown this awful curse. The Roman Catholic Church decreed in 1957 that this teaching of eternal Jewish guilt to every Christian child must stop.

Messianic claims

In these last years much progress has been made toward restoring a less propagandistic knowledge of Jesus. For the Jew, the moral, ethical, and spiritual teachings of Jesus do not even raise the problem of Christianity. It is the church creed as it grew, outside of Jerusalem, that is the problem.

First came the question of accepting Jesus

Auto da fé, or "act of faith," was the euphemism by which Inquisitors designated the burning alive of Jews who would not abjure their faith. This painting hangs in the Prado, Madrid.

as the Messiah. In his own words, as reported in the Gospels, Jesus tells his followers that they who are standing listening to him will see the kingdom established within their own lifetime. Obviously this did not happen, so the Jews as a whole regarded Jesus as one more Messiah who had failed.

There were others. To be considered the Messiah in those days meant to be the bringer of freedom, and this usually meant to be the leader of revolt. We know from the parchments found in the great excavation at Masada that even the Essenes, whom scholars until then had believed to be pacifists, had men among the secret resistance fighters. We have the tragic example only sixty years after the Temple was destroyed of Bar Kokhba gathering resistance groups, and of the octogenarian sage, Rabbi Akiva, hailing Bar Kokhba as the Messiah. Thus Jesus, to most Jews, was another Messiah tragically proven wrong. But this prophet had an amazing effect on his close followers, so amazing that they constructed a religion around his story that was to sweep a vast part of the world.

We may easily become confused about Christianity and Judaism if we stop at the fact that Jesus was a devout Jew and that the first Christians were synagogue Jews. For then, some argue, the teachings of Jesus are a "continuation of Judaism," and why shouldn't Jews accept them? In the main, those teachings were already a part of Judaism and were and are accepted. What the Jews cannot accept is the idolatry that grew around the image of Jesus. What the Jews cannot accept is the divinity of Jesus, a man. To Judaism this is not a progression, but a regression to the pagan cults against which Abraham revolted. As has often been said, Jesus himself could not have accepted this. He did not claim to be the "Son of God"; he announced himself as the "son of man," as *ben Adam*, and this is a common way of describing a man simply as one of the people.

Christian dogma and rites

How, then, did Christianity change all this, and spread? Why did people in far places from Africa to Ireland care about the story of a preacher in a small country who was unjustly executed? Countless other Jews, countless other rebels and slaves in many Roman-occupied lands, were crucified. What gave this case such a hold on world imagination?

The story, with all its miracle tales, was carried into lands where people were still worshiping stone gods, and spirits, and emperors. The story as it grew and changed linked itself to some of their ancient beliefs, such as the Greek mythological belief that gods came down on earth and begot sons. Thus came the curious admixture, the story of a birth through a virgin united with a spirit, the Holy Spirit that was an emanation of the Godhead. God was One, the One was Three—God, the Holy Spirit, and the Son of God. This trinity became the central belief in the Christian creed.

But it was not only this echo of gods coming down on earth that attracted converts. The most powerful hold of the new religion was through promise of heaven and fear of hell. Of lesser importance in the new teaching was life on earth, which in Judaism is the center.

While Judaism had pictured heaven and hell simply as illustrations for good and bad, the new religion emphasized the afterlife completely, offering the exclusive chance of eternal salvation to those who joined. What were a few mortal years compared to a joyous eternity? And if one did not become baptized, why, then, this meant eternal suffering in hell. Even babies who died before they could be baptized were doomed, if not to hell, then to endless limbo.

This threatening idea came from what was called "original sin." The story of Adam and Eve was given as proof that after the sin of Adam, all mankind forever was "born in sin." The sin of birth, or of being born, could be washed away only by the symbolic act of baptism by a priest of the new religious cult. It was conceded that a right-minded person *might* be in state of "natural grace." But baptismal initiation into Christianity, and this alone, could give a person reasonable likelihood of being saved from unending damnation. Whether he then went to heaven or hell depended on his faith and conduct all throughout his life. For Jesus had died on the cross as a sacrifice for the sins of mankind, so as to make salvation possible for those who believed this.

The Christian must also believe in Judgment Day, when Jesus, sitting on the right hand of God, would judge for eternity all who had ever lived, for on that day everyone would be raised from the dead to stand before God and His Son. Although Judaism contains this image of the Messiah, it is not, of course, a dogma.

The Annunciation scene has been depicted by many Christian painters—here by the Flemish Jan Van Eyck (fifteenth century).

We can readily see that such dogma was far from the ethical simplicity of Judaism. Christianity developed other ceremonial rites, besides the initiation of baptism. One of the most important was called the *eucharist*. This ceremony recalls the last supper, or Seder, at which Jesus is pictured as offering the wine cup to his disciples, saying, "This is my blood," and portions of the *matzah*, saying, "This is my flesh." From this came the service called *mass*. In the Christian mass, the priest, and in some churches the communicant also, sips wine; a wafer is given to the communicant. In the Catholic Church, according to a doctrine called *transubstantiation*, the wine and wafer are believed to be mystically transformed into the blood and body of Jesus. The communicants "receiving" them are believed to have entered into a special spiritual relationship with the Son of God.

The leadership of Paul

None of this seems to have existed in the normal Jewish belief of the disciples, led by the brother of Jesus in Jerusalem. The cult was developed outside of Jerusalem by a curious, remarkable organizer named Paul, who extended the Christian church to non-Jews. Who was Paul? Originally known as Saul of Tarsus, a Jewish nationalist, although a Roman citizen, he was a man who had absorbed Greek ideas but still followed Jewish law and rites. His first contact with the Jesus sect was as a prosecutor. Small groups of believers in Jesus had formed in various synagogues, still hoping for the Messiah to

return to life and free the Jews from the Romans. They were considered dangerous, and Saul, according to his own account, was sent by the chief priest to arrest such a group in Damascus. On the road to Damascus he was struck by a vision of Jesus asking him, "Why do you persecute me?"

So powerful was this guilt-ridden experience that Saul was blinded for several days. The very same people whom he had intended to arrest in Damascus helped him; he was converted, changed his name to Paul, and began to travel around the Mediterranean, teaching his faith in Jesus as the Messiah. When not enough Jews listened, he told the story to gentiles. He excused them from circumcision and the Sabbath laws.

A split grew between Paul and the leaders of the early church in Jerusalem. They, he charged, knew nothing beyond the baptism that had already been practiced by John, before Jesus. When the Jerusalem church was destroyed, Pauline Christianity dominated the movement. Its adaptations to the ways and needs of suffering populations to whom it offered the hope of a better afterlife brought growth.

A complex church history

The history of the Christian Church is complex. Some views were disputed, changed. But the central dogma remains, that Jesus is the only Son of God, who was conceived by the Holy Spirit and born of the Virgin Mary, crucified, died and was buried, and rose on the third day, ascended to heaven, and will come again, in judgment of the living and of the dead.

In some times and places Jews have been made to wear distinguishing badges or special garb. These Jews, shown in a post-Byzantine icon, wore conical hats and round badges in conformity with a decree issued by Pope Innocent III.

Power in the church eventually was divided between Rome and the Eastern Orthodox factions. There were differences between them in liturgy, and there were different shadings of dogma, which, though subtle, served to arouse deep controversy. Furthermore, the Orthodox church, in Russia, Greece, and other countries, allowed their priests, though not their bishops, to marry; the Roman Catholics did not permit this. This is a question which remained a center of dispute and one which has reappeared in our time.

In the sixteenth century, followers of Martin Luther created the Protestant movement in which marriage of priests was permitted; Protestants objected to the worship of saints, as a violation of the commandment against idolatry, and to the selling of indulgences, by which Christians could be freed of sin, for repentance *and* a payment. But all these are questions within the Christian movement.

Our Jewish concern is with life conduct, and with activities for human betterment, where Christians and Jews have teachings in common. Our concern also is to help Christianity rid itself totally of hostility to Jews. Although Jews have been victims of certain Christian movements in the past, we all know, also, of the great sacrifices that were made by individual Christians to save Jewish lives, particularly during the Nazi holocaust. And we all know that the Christian ideal is a spiritual one that can rise to the highest purity and intensity. We respect all religious faith, for in every faith man is seeking to reach God—even as we are, in ours.

15 Has the world gone beyond religion?

You have been taught that to live an ethical life is the highest way to practice your religion. Judaism places good acts above smoke from the altar, above acts of formal worship. You express your love of God through your love for your neighbor. Further, you have been taught that various religions arrive at the same Golden Rule, the same knowledge of the Oneness of God, the same sense of universal purpose. Christianity and Judaism, you have long known, share the same original Bible, and Christian worship even shares many of our prayers. From this you may at first have thought that it makes little difference which religion you follow. Your second thought may have been that you need follow no religion at all, since you can behave ethically, you can be charitable, you can love your neighbor, and do justly, and show mercy, without going to a synagogue, without saying prayers, or having a Seder on Passover.

You may even go over in your mind the ways of people whom you know, both young people and older, who do not worship in any religion, and yet who lead ethical lives. Perhaps organized religion has ended its mission? Perhaps those who simply be-

130

lieve in a universal God and in furthering human good should be excused as "graduated"?

Possibly you hesitate to express these thoughts, sometimes even to yourself, for they seem disloyal. But it is best to think them through.

The secular approach

The idea that all of the ethical advice of modern religions can be carried out in daily life without religious connection is called the "secular approach." In present-day governments, particularly in democracies, there are laws that carry out the social demands of the Ten Commandments. "I am thy God" is of course omitted; no one has by law to believe in God, and there is no public law against worshiping idols, but our social laws and our criminal laws deal with all the other commandments. They protect a day of rest, they punish blasphemy, they extend social security to our elders, they forbid murder, stealing, adultery, bearing false witness, and they discourage covetousness.

Our many social movements open the way for charities and for good deeds toward our neighbors. What is left for religion? What is left for God? Not long ago a slogan swept the intellectual world: God is dead. It was really in reaction to a world of atomic warfare, race riots, drug addiction, hunger, and assassination. It meant that God was "dead" or absent in mankind. That was the hopeless side of the slogan. What some of the more atheistic people meant was that the very idea of God was a dead issue, and that Com-

munism or other social movements could take over and accomplish the same ends that religions had sought in God, that men could arrive at social justice without the idea of God.

The failure of materialistic methods

If all our messianic ideals, if all our social teaching, can be accomplished without God, where then is the place of religion, and if there remains a place—why one religion rather than another?

On the first part of that question, we might remember that this "if" is still a big supposition.

Some secularists want simply to put their trust in man, hoping as Rabbi Eugene Borowitz says, "that if he were brought up in a noncompetitive social order his innate goodness would assert itself." But to this hope, Rabbi Borowitz raises some objections:

If religion must live in a world where scientific doubts have been raised by Copernicus, Darwin, Marx, Freud, and Einstein, then secularism lives in a world that has seen Auschwitz, Hiroshima, Babi Yar, Sharpeville, Selma, Detroit, and Watts —to name only the most obvious cases. This is no century in which to appeal to the natural goodness of men.

In other words, we are far, far from ready at this time to trust social motivation alone. We cannot even foresee the time when we can do so, and give up the urging of religion. Suppose we look at those nations that have tried to efface religion and depend entirely on the materialistic method to bring society into messianic times. What do we see? Suppression, and war, and brutal injustices still in force. And all this is combined with a dreadful sense of spiritual emptiness and deprivation. After half a century of anti-religious education, going through three generations, people still cling to and search for a higher motivation in their lives. This can only be recognized as a religious need, for in every one of us there is a recognition of the gap between man's knowledge and the infinite.

The fiftieth door

This gap is referred to in a saying of the Baal Shem Tov about Moses.

We read in the Talmud that forty-nine doors of understanding out of fifty were opened to Moses. But since man always aspires to know still more, how did Moses continue his search for understanding? When he found the fiftieth door closed to him, because this is the door that is unapproachable to the human mind, Moses accepted that the final knowledge was faith, and turned again to meditate on those other phases of knowledge that were open to him.

Thus with every man [said the Baal Shem], when man has reached a point beyond which he is unable to comprehend, then he must study more deeply the learning within his grasp. Beyond a certain point, both the sage and the ignorant man are alike.

Beyond a certain point in human social action this is also true, and even the most sophisticated person will find himself inwardly praying for guidance or fortitude, or calling up to his help some prophetic, religious cry, out of the depths of our covenant with God.

Need for divine wisdom

The pattern of justice is not as clear as the atomic table. Each human situation brings ethical questions into play, so that we long for some divine wisdom to help us know, in each choice we make in life, what is truly good and right. Let us take a most obvious question: How should a murderer be sentenced? If he killed for money, but came from a life of ignorance and poverty? If he killed out of jealousy? If he assassinated out of patriotism? Our social structure is at best a man-made machine, and we yearn for a feeling of spiritual clarity each time we are called upon to make a social, or secular, decision.

Great scientists, particularly physicists, have again and again recognized the fiftieth door of Moses and avowed the place of religion in modern society. Some, as would be characteristic, indicate this as a universal religion. Our own Albert Einstein repeatedly paired Jewish and Christian ethical teachings, saying, "the highest principles for our aspirations and judgments are given to us in Jewish-Christian religious tradition." He did not regard himself as an observant Jew, but was profoundly and actively attached to Judaism. He spoke devotedly of Zionism in terms of a "need for a spiritual center for the Jews."

Personal and communal worship

The great personality, the creative genius, may find his own way to express his reli-

This French Jew was expressing the spirit of worship in formal prayer and ritual observance. It is also expressed in the striving to be and do good.

gious feelings, and stay apart from communal worship. Indeed, Martin Buber was not a synagogue-goer, but who would doubt the primary place of religion in society, from his works? Human society has been structured around religion from the first awakening of man's sense of awe, from the first recognition of conscience. Now and in the foreseeable future we still depend—and will depend—on organized religion to guide us ethically in each situation as it arises. That is why we see religious leaders taking part in every social action, where political leaders are often rare.

Man may dream of a totally personal form of worship, and even practice it in his soul. But he finds he can only live his spiritual life actively, among men, through the community of religion. In much the same way he may dream of a utopian society in which he is free to do all that he wishes, of a government that interferes so little in his life that it hardly exists—and yet he finds that he must be part of our organized society, in order to do the things he wants to do.

The three faiths in America

Today in America religion has, in a sense, been allotted its place. In the typical suburban community, for example, we see the familiar three-faith pattern, Protestant Church, Catholic Church, and Synagogue. Indeed, people seem to fear that the "equality" of the three faiths, even their common ethical views, will reduce the belief in each.

Yet if we look at the secular structure of

society, we see a reassuring parallel. We do not fear, for example, that the common democratic beliefs of the French, the English, and the Americans will weaken each one's belief in democracy. Each people finds its way to its truth through its own history, culture, and continuity. So does each faith find its way to God.

Are we Jews simply then "another faith"? Are we to use for ourselves, and for the deepest meaning of our Jewishness, that discouraging, common term, "one of the . . ."? Are we "one of the" three most prominent American faiths and thereby diminished in the uniqueness of our spiritual life?

Each of the others asks the same question. Each of the others concludes that for its own people the illumination provided by its own faith is the great revealing light. This too is part of the mysterious gap between man and a final understanding of creation.

Covenant and purpose

Where, then, is our "chosenness"? If we tend to think of it or describe it in terms of superiority we know we are not justified, for the Talmud tells us that knowledge of God is given to all flesh. But the choice, as Judaism accepts it, was and is a covenant, an agreement between God and man, revealed and perceived in our Jewish tradition and kept by us as a continuing society, no matter how other groups should conceive their relationship to God. In our covenant, God shows man what is right, and man by his individual will should choose to do it. Without the part of man, the part of God can cease to exist.

Without man's choice of act upon act, the movement of history, that mysterious mission of creation, cannot go forward. And so we were chosen, and we chose to do.

It is a community of men that receives and acts out the covenant, each as an individual, all as a collectivity, and through history as a continuation, studying, interpreting, adding. Only Judaism can provide this to us, the Jews, as a collective experience.

Out of the awareness, on our part, of a moral God, came other awareness, to other people—both Christianity and Islam, which have spread to multitudes of people. When such great movements, each with its particular illuminations, have been engendered from the revelation and choice that our people experienced, can we doubt that choice called chosenness?

Some Jews take the spread of these ethical concepts, and of the teachings of our patriarchs and prophets, to be a self-evident proof of all the claims ever made for a kind of superiority in the Jewish people. Others feel that we are simply an instrument chosen in this part of the universal purpose. We remain in awe at the unfolding mystery, at the unparalleled events that continue to bring revelations through us. We have seen both the holocaust and the rebirth of Israel in recent times. These, too, are events in our Jewish portion of revelation.

The sanctification of life

We may again consider the view of Einstein, for in our scientific age he is, to many, the very symbol of rational idealism.

Judaism is not a creed. The Jewish God is simply the negation of superstition . . . Judaism is concerned with life as we live it and as we can, to a certain extent, grasp it, and nothing else. . . . It seems to me, therefore, doubtful whether it can be called a religion in the accepted sense of the word, particularly as no "faith" but the santification of life in a suprapersonal sense is demanded of the Jew.

But the Jewish religion also contains something else, something which finds special expression in many of the Psalms, namely, a sort of intoxicated joy and amazement at the beauty and grandeur of the world, of which man can form just a faint notion. This joy is the feeling from which true scientific research draws its spiritual sustenance. . . .

Is what I have described a distinguishing mark of Judaism? Is it to be found anywhere else under another name? In its pure form, it is nowhere to be found, not even in Judaism, where the pure doctrine is obscured by much worship of the letter. Yet Judaism seems to me to be one of its purest and most vigorous manifestations. This applies particularly to the fundamental principle of the sanctification of life.

It is characteristic that the animals were expressly included in the command to keep holy the Sabbath day, so strong was the feeling of the ideal solidarity of all living things. The insistence on the solidarity of all human beings finds still stronger expression, and it is no mere chance that the demands of Socialism were for the most part raised by Jews.

How strongly developed this sense of the sanctity of life is in the Jewish people is admirably illustrated by a little remark which Walter Rathenau once made to me in conversation: "When a Jew says that he's going hunting to amuse himself, he lies." The Jewish sense of the sanctity of life could not be more simply expressed.

Albert Einstein, Nobel Prize physicist and father of the theory of relativity. The honored scientist fled Nazi Germany in 1933 and came to the United States.

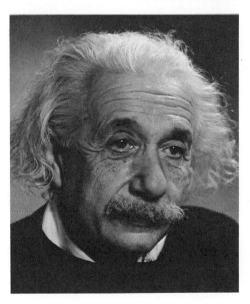

In speaking of the "intoxicated joy and amazement at the beauty and grandeur of the world," is Einstein so far from the Ḥasidim?

In modern, materialist society, religion is needed, some feel, more than ever as the constant urge toward this sanctification. Some persons feel this urge most strongly through ritual, through the joined experience of a congregation, others feel it through works that they undertake. But, like Moses, all may turn for greater understanding to the doors that have already been opened to us. Religious study is not reserved for scholars but is the concern of every man of conscience.

It may well be observed that the religious motive has at times failed mankind, has at times been used for betrayal, just as it has at other times led to the highest beauty and joy. There remains no other structure in human society, and no other urge, that can so help man to gratify his hunger to realize the sanctity of life.

Jewish hopes, Jewish duties

16 How can we tell right from wrong?

Why should we need religion, anymore, to help us tell right from wrong? And why should Jews need the Jewish religion for this? After all, there are laws in every country. There are courses in ethics. And if we get too confused, psychiatrists will tell us there is usually no such thing as an objective "right" or "wrong."

Applying the commandments

Perhaps the oldest laws in common use today go back to the basic code of the Ten Commandments, but from laws enforced by the power or authority of religion we have gone over to civil laws that are supposed to keep us from doing wrong.

And yet with all these laws, religious as well as civil, to guide us, we are sometimes perplexed, as we make decisions at every moment of our lives, about what is right and what is wrong. Laws reaching all the way from the Ten Commandments to our city ordinances tell us it is wrong to steal. But is it wrong for an agent who is serving his country to steal military secrets?

That may be a television-story type of

problem which few of us have to deal with in life. But here is one that is closer to us: It is wrong to lie, but is it wrong to tell a "white lie" to keep someone from having needless pain? On a small, daily scale, is it wrong to tell a social lie, like "I'm sorry, but I have another engagement," when you are invited by someone you don't want to see? Or, is holding back the truth a lie, as when a doctor does not tell a cancer patient he is doomed?

We all know that what might be right in one time and place may be wrong in another, but how are we to judge? Is there one over-all guideline that helps us make these constant, and delicate judgments?

Bad and good impulses

From the early days in Judaism we are given explanations that speak of the "bad urge" and the "good urge," the *yetzer ha-ra,* and the *yetzer ha-tov.*

According to Jewish tradition, the bad urge is with us from birth. One is considered fully responsible for standing ever against it when he has reached Bar Mitzvah age, that is, the age of judgment and social responsibility. In modern thinking, let us say in psychoanalysis, the "urge" might correspond to the *id,* the deep, animal desire which some scientists now even claim has a source in a kind of vestigial reptilian brain that remains in us. This urge is not always necessarily "bad," but exists without distinction of good or bad. The instinct to take food may cause a hungry child to steal. With a grown-up person, we would sympathize if

hunger made him steal, yet there are many stories of people who starved but would not steal. A complex system of right-and-wrong had been absorbed by them. There are many variations on such values, and we want to know what are the most helpful for us.

As we grow and recognize the rights and needs of other people, we develop a sense of ourselves, an ego, and beyond that a conscience, called the *superego.* This is closest to what is meant by the good urge. In some social systems and in some religions it is fenced in, or conditioned very strongly, so that very little self-judgment remains. Yet the nature of the superego is such that most people feel that they can recognize, in themselves what is right.

Judaism warns us somewhat about this. We are told that the *yetzer ha-ra* is always there. The Talmud remarks, "The evil impulse is first like a passer-by, then like a lodger, and finally like a master in the house." Against this, Judaism stresses the moral sense. Not all codes have left man so much responsibility of judgment. The reverse was true of the codes of ancient Rome, where the letter of the law was sufficient.

Moral and civil law

Today in America, our civil laws recognize that there is a difference between civil and moral laws—not only for Jews but for people of all religions. When a draft board has to decide whether a man is truly a pacifist, he usually must prove he is a "conscientious objector" by his religion. Only recently has this rule been questioned, since it makes no provision for the nonreligious pacifist. But the fact that the government, with all its laws, could not decide on a question of conscience, and declared this was a religious matter, shows how the most important decisions in our lives about right and wrong are still deeply connected with religious teaching. That is what we commonly understand as "a higher law." Not all countries, of course, take this view.

Professor Salo Baron points out that we can see the dividing line between civil and moral laws as far back as Moses, for at Sinai Moses proclaimed not only a set of moral laws, the Commandments, but also a set of very detailed regulations about what should or should not be eaten, about inheritance, and many more. Now, the day-to-day regulations, even though included at that time under a religious authority, were more like civil laws, and could be adapted as social life changed. But the moral laws are fundamental guides.

For example, "Thou shalt not bear false witness" is a moral law as well as a civil law. In civil law, "bearing false witness" becomes perjury in a trial, but few of us are often called upon to be courtroom witnesses. The moral law serves far more broadly. Repeating gossip or slander is a daily possibility, and here the moral law helps each person decide when to keep from spreading tales.

A unifying rule

It is unfortunately true that many people consider they are right, simply if they do not break any civil law. That is why among

Collective problems need collective action. Jews have been leaders in unions such as the Amalgamated Clothing Workers, shown here in a 1947 parade for the rights of labor.

Jews for many generations there were people who felt extremely righteous because they kept the 613 *mitzvot* or ordinances ascribed to the Torah, and yet among them were certainly to be found persons who were not what we would feel to be "good people." One can learn to live strictly within the letter of the law and still be unjust, ungenerous, deceitful, and hurtful.

To help us to get away from this tendency to say we were right because we broke no laws, the question of good and bad, right and wrong, has been compacted into rules even simpler than the Ten Commandments.

Just as in physics, Einstein always searched for the single unifying equation, the unified field theory, that explained all the laws of nature, so in human conduct there has been a search for the unifying rule to help ourselves tell good from bad.

Ernest Hemingway tried to make such a rule for himself. He said, "What makes me feel good is good." Of course we might not accept this from the Marquis de Sade. People admired this concept from Hemingway because his writing showed him to be a sensitive person who wanted to be decent to others. He meant he knew he was being decent when he felt good about the way he was behaving. He meant that the modern person should not obey rules blindly, but should choose through the test of his own "feeling good about it" what was good or bad. He was saying that each person should be finely tuned to his *yetzer ha-tov*.

Yet we can see the dangers of this rule. A killer may feel "good" when he kills, and say therefore he is justified. This is almost always the case with political assassins.

Hemingway's rule may only be a kind of modern moral shorthand for the Golden Rule that was stated by Moses, Confucius, Jesus, and doubtless by prophets in other religions. It has several forms: "Love thy neighbor as thyself," the way it appears in the Books of Moses, "Do not do to others what you do not like yourself," the way Confucius and Hillel put it, and as put by Jesus, "Do unto others what you would have them do unto you."

This rule can indeed be used as a guide for almost any situation in which we find ourselves. It is like a listening aid, for hearing the *yetzer ha-tov* over the *yetzer ha-ra*. And yet, though this rule has been known over thousands of years in various great civilizations, it has not brought us to the perfect society, by any means.

While there must have been tens of millions of people who did live good lives through using this rule, we have not yet achieved a society that lives by it. We still need to hear and to *do* the right—not only individually but collectively, as ethical persons in ethically oriented governments and societies.

The philosophers' approach

Many people think the search for a unifying rule that will guide mankind is not necessarily a religious matter. Great philosophers, some of them not at all religious, have also tried to find the single rule of judging right from wrong. The German philosopher Immanuel Kant, called it the "categorical imperative," or "the thing you must do." "Act in such a way," he wrote, "that you treat humanity, both in your own person and in others, never as a means but always also as an end." First of all, this formula includes the Golden Rule, since we are told to act the same for our own person as for others. But it adds the consideration of humanity as a whole, above the people who may be involved at the moment. Every action we take should be weighed not only for its immediate effect on ourselves, on our friends, and on our neighbors, but also for its end effect on humanity as a whole.

That might be taken to mean human destiny, or creation, or messianic times, or the intention of God.

Differing emphases

Now if a nonreligious philosopher can give us such a guide, and if several great teachers, some of them far from Jewish, offer us the same Golden Rule, how does Judaism particularly help us?

Perhaps the key word is "us." We are not Confucians, to be helped through that civilization, nor are we Christians; we are Jews.

Walter Kaufmann, a teacher of philosophy at Princeton, writes that it is basically incorrect, even if we find the Golden Rule repeated, to say that different religions teach the same morality, for when they tell how to behave under that rule, they are divided. "It is fashionable to say that all the religious teachers of mankind have taught the same morality," he writes, ". . . but it is obvious that they have *not*. . . . Many of the Hebrew prophets were centrally concerned with social justice. Jesus, Paul, Luther, Calvin, Laotze and the Buddha were not." While this

Individual study problems yield to the one-to-one approach. This young tutor and his pupil are taking part in the tutorial program of the New York Mitzvah Corps of the National Federation of Temple Youth (affiliated with the UAHC).

statement might enrage good Christians, what he means is that "sin" in some religions has more emphasis than social justice.

Besides, different religions teach very different reactions to situations of right and wrong. The Christian teaching of "turn the other cheek," as we have already noted, is to the Jew not an acceptable response, particularly today. The Buddhist attitude of letting things pass does not suit us either. The Muslim conception, used even today, of carrying out "the will of Allah" through "a holy war," a *jihad,* cannot be consistent with the Golden Rule.

The godliness of life

It is perhaps the added objective, the question of eventual value to humanity, stated in Kant's rule, that comes closest to the special meaning of Judaism. It is humanity as an end, a goal, that he asks us to consider. What is "good" is what advances that idea. This is in our tradition of messianic times, of universal justice, of the spiritual godliness of life. This is the idea that has inspired Judaism, the idea of a covenant, a taking part with God in His doing on earth.

Rabbi Leo Baeck, who perfected his thinking during years in the concentration camp at Theresienstadt, wrote, "Some Jews seem to think that Judaism is completely contained in the ethical commandments and that the belief in God is a mere adornment. A grosser superficiality could not possibly be inflicted on the Jewish religion." For the gap between a stated law, even a Kantian rule, and our will to apply it in every situation in life, can only be bridged by that

"urge" called the *yetzer ha-tov.* It is a command on the side of the good.

For Judaism, Baeck says, "the essential nature of its ethics is that they are commandments of God." Only to obey rules and statutes would be "mere moralism."

This is why the interpretation of right and wrong, good and bad, has gone on and on among our rabbis and our people, through the centuries, often with equal-sounding arguments on both sides of a question, but always with the spirit of seeking what is the higher good. There is an accumulation and a continuity in this, to which our spirit responds as we grow up in contact with the Jewish way of life. At times, in the cosmopolitan world, a wisdom-saying from the Buddha, or even a godless philosopher's rule, or a poet's word, may, like Hemingway's personal code, help us to tell right from wrong at a given moment. Yet in the dreadfully complex decisions, in questions of war, in questions of social justice, civil rights, even in the complexities of voting in an election, where loyalty to a political party or a friend may weigh against a better policy, no ready rule of thumb will help.

The Jewish belief is in each person's own relationship to the godly impulse, or as the Ḥasidim put it—in the spark of godliness in each of us. It is the individual who must decide, while at every moment counseled from both sides, by the evil urge and the good urge, by the primeval flow of energy and the spiritualizing force of conscience, backed by his total culture. Each Jew must explore, and call up, in difficult problems of right and wrong, everything that the Jewish experience can offer him.

17 What can the Ten Commandments mean to us today?

In all the codes and constitutions that man has sought to obey, none has been as widely known, admired, and generally accepted—even if rarely completely followed—as the code of the Ten Commandments. As Lewis Browne observed in *The Wisdom of Israel,* there is no other single document of the law to compare with it for brevity, comprehensiveness, forcefulness and high ethical and moral character.

A measuring rod

So deeply is this code imbedded in human society that we measure our actions by it a thousand times a day. When we are uncertain whether it is the good or evil urge that prompts us, we usually check it in our souls against the Commandments.

True, there are other guides. For instance, there is the single, universal law, contained in the Books of Moses, which tells us to love our neighbors as ourselves—a code that would in itself embrace the human relations in the Commandments. It would tell us not to murder, lie, commit adultery, covet, steal, and to respect father and mother. The Commandments spell out these admonitions. Further, the Golden Rule might not serve, for it would not teach us about God, would not forbid the worship of idols, and would not raise the Sabbath to a day of holiness.

In modern times, with the accent on materialism, some people may well feel that the social commandments are enough, that we do not need to identify God, that we do not need to be forbidden to worship statues, that the six-day and even the five-day week ensure us days for rest and meditation.

But the concept of the Ten Commandments has such a profound place in our society that it is well to trace its meaning to see if it surmounts the legalistic view.

Let us turn to the same writer, Lewis Browne, a modern rabbi who through the greater part of his career did not lead a congregation but through his popular writings fulfilled the rabbi's role of teacher. He reminds us that the original code was put into ten laws "perhaps in order to help the primitive herdsmen memorize the Commandments by ticking them off on the fingers of their two hands." This might also be an explanation for the division of the Commandments onto two tablets.

But when the Jew of those times ticked off the Ten Commandments on his fingers, just as you might mentally do today, was he thinking of them as tribal laws, for which there were definite punishments? We today have, on our legal books, punishments for murder, for theft, for perjury, for adultery, even for violations of the Sabbath, and for "taking the name of God in vain"—swearing. Some of these, like the laws about swearing, are often called "dead-letter laws" because customs have changed so that they are rarely enforced.

Brooding Mount Sinai, clad in a smoky mist, recalls the solemn day of "thou shalt" and "thou shalt not"—the receiving of the commandments, promises by which God bound a people to Himself.

An "I-Thou" relationship

But though the Ten Commandments deal very much with the same subjects, they are not tribal, or community, ordinances. True, many of the Commandments were put into the form of ordinances, in the long list of tribal laws in the Bible, but this does not seem to be the way the Commandments themselves were meant to be taken. For as Martin Buber said, they are uttered by an I and addressed to a thou. An "I" commands, and a thou, every person who hears this "thou," is commanded.

And each of us is still such a thou. What we hear is the conscience-command from on high; this is the ultimate *yetzer ha-tov*, the Godhead, speaking to the soul of each man.

He who issues the command, Buber points out, has no executive power. Society may later break down the commands into laws and appoint policemen and courts and judges. But if we consider the commands in their pure state, as brought down by Moses from Mount Sinai, they are given in an I-Thou relationship. Whoever does not wish to respond to the "thou" addressed to him, Buber tells us, can apparently go about his business unimpeded. He who rejects the I is not struck down by lightning, and he who accepts the voice does not find hidden treasures. Religions later on may tell us such things, but in that very first meeting there is only faith, the faith of man in God.

Isn't this the way we understand the conscience of man, today?

Judaism has always understood the Ten Commandments in this way. In his book, *Legends of the Bible*, drawn mostly from Midrashic sources, the great scholar Louis Ginzberg tells us:

These words . . . made known by God on Mount Sinai, were heard not by Israel alone, but by the inhabitants of all the earth. The Divine voice divided itself into all the seventy tongues of men, so that all might understand it . . . When the Divine voice sounded, all the dead in Sheoul were revived, and betook themselves to Sinai; . . . yea, even the souls of those who had not yet been born were present. Every prophet, every sage, received at Sinai his share of the revelation, which in the course of history was to be announced by them to mankind. All heard indeed the same words, but the same voice, corresponding to the individuality of each, was God's way of speaking with them.

Interwoven laws

The Ten Commandments are so closely interwoven, the same author reminds us, that the breaking of one leads to the breaking of another. We may readily see how the laws interweave, in speaking to us in our own time. The first is the declaration of God, "I am the God that brought Thee out of slavery in Egypt." In our times, even those who reject a formal religion still call in times of agony for some unknowable power to free them from the tormenting inner slaveries that demean, from enslavement to character faults, from enslavement to social forces inwardly despised, from all forms of compulsion. To surmount the Egypt within ourselves, we call for strength, for the "outstretched arm" that brought each man, each "thou" out of slavery.

And this commandment is directly linked to the second, against the making of images, to bow down before them. In our times, in despair of following our own conscience, men may set up images of all-powerful leaders, and worship them—images of a Hitler, a Stalin, or even an image of Science. This has actually taken place in modern times. Though the fact is not widely publicized, Hitler, in his attacks on Christianity, took over a few Protestant churches and forcibly had his picture installed in them for worship—as the leader of a kind of Germanic neo-paganism. Mao is actively worshiped today.

And although we see that a man simply cannot give up his conscience to a ruler, or to an idea, there is still the danger of expecting God to respond to our every request. And so we enchain onto the third commandment, not to take the name of God in vain. For to call on God for personal service would be to reduce God to the state of an idol, and again to try to evade our human responsibility. To swear falsely, by the name of God, would be even worse. Clearly, in violating the third commandment, one violates both the second and the first. Thus the first three are linked, and may be viewed as a single command of reverence joined with responsibility.

Holiness of the Sabbath

It is the fourth commandment, regarding the Sabbath, that seems so specific as to have

no link with the others. While the first three are broad, basic, and self-evident if man is to seek God at all, the fourth sounds more like a regulation. It tells us to keep the Sabbath day holy. Six days are workdays, and on the seventh a man may not work, neither you, nor your son, nor your daughter, nor your male or female slave, nor the stranger who lives in your settlement, nor any of your cattle, nor anyone whom you employ, and who lives in your community.

This sounds like a bylaw that has somehow been elevated to a place amongst the Commandments. And we know that from the specific clauses in this Commandment, Judaism developed a complex series of laws that at times seemed to govern an entire culture.

The logical mind asks, Why a Sabbath at all? Suppose a man likes to work on his own rhythm, suppose he prefers to reserve certain hours each day for contemplation and rest? or a week out of each two months? Is that any less holy than dividing his time according to an ancient taboo? Indeed, the complex organization of modern society makes it impossible for everyone to cease work on the same day.

First, let us take the highest explanation for the Sabbath, the one that links man to God. The story of Genesis tells us that God created the world and man in six days and on the seventh day He rested. As man is created in God's image, the Sabbath rule is an affirmation of this link, and of the mystical idea that each soul is a "spark" of God; therefore man repeats the divine pattern with a seventh day of rest.

But we may reply that we do not believe in the anthropomorphic way of thinking that makes man a tiny imitation of God. We may regard the entire creation story as poetic.

The ideal of equality

Yet there is another meaning in the Sabbath Commandment that elevates it to a place among the great moral pronouncements: it is a commandment of equality. In the social order where there were still masters and slaves, the Commandment establishes one area of equality. For our understanding today, this raises social law to the level of religious and moral law.

We know that for the Sabbath in former times, Jews developed an atmosphere of beauty and holiness that seems impossible for us to retrieve, and that this richness and enjoyment fully balanced, for them, any inconvenience in their strict Sabbath laws. Some people raised the question whether such inconveniences are really necessary to the enjoyment of Sabbath. There are modern Jews who say Yes as well as those who say No. The writer Herman Wouk says in *This Is My God:*

The American Jew, by taking thought and pains, by keeping the Sabbath over the years, by accepting difficulties for the sake of the results, can have what the Sabbath offers. He has to work at it more than his fathers did, with a lower charge of religious energy. It is a hard case. That the Sabbath should be the usual breaking-off point from tradition is perhaps inevitable. It is also the point at which many Jews rejoin Judaism. Probably it is the natural and best point.

To those who oppose Wouk's view, a meticulous observance of the Sabbath is in itself slavish, and at times hypocritical. For example, the practice of using a "Shabbes goy" to light the fire or to perform other chores forbidden on the "day of rest" smacks of hypocrisy, and some of the mechanical devices that are used to circumvent strict regulations smack of the ridiculous. For example, in some hotels for the Orthodox in Tel Aviv, Jerusalem, and New York as well, there are automatic elevators that keep going up and down all through the Sabbath, stopping at every floor, so that no one has to violate the day of rest by pushing a button.

While circumventional "legal fictions" are understood as such among the observant, their antagonists find grounds for the moral question as to whether systems of subterfuge, or legalistic-minded evasions of what are taken to be God's laws, do not in themselves create a type of mind that does not match up to the high moral concepts of Judaism. And so they ask—do we want to win against God on technicalities, so as to have our comforts while we pretend to put them aside?

Ordinances—and interpretations

Perhaps the difficulty is not in the Sabbath Commandment itself but in confusing it with all the ordinances that have been devised and attached to it. When our Orthodox forefathers came to America the question of having to work on Saturday was for many a tragic one. And yet, the early Talmudists were not inflexible. If a man is lost in the desert, they said, and forgets what day it is, let him then count six days and observe the seventh as the Sabbath. It is the great principle of rest and renewal, of a time of contemplation and joy that is meant by the Sabbath.

In one way, the material progress of man has taken the tension out of this specific problem. Where the Orthodox Jewish immigrant had to make a heart-searching decision, the Jew of today who chooses to keep Saturday and not Sunday as his holy day of rest, is unlikely to have any problem. The shorter work week takes the hardship out of the choice. And it is true that the atmosphere of a Sabbath eve at home, in particular, is being brought back more and more, sought after by Jews who had "dropped it all" only to find themselves with a sense of emptiness and loss.

We have dwelt on the Fourth Commandment because it is the one that is most questioned. It is, if one wishes, the most cultic one, in the way it has come down to us. As with the kosher laws, a great range of adjustment has taken place, and despite what was feared, this has not brought an end to Judaism.

Honor to parents

The Fifth Commandment, again, is one that does not seem to belong to the same concept as the others. It seems so natural and self-evident that a person should honor his father and mother, that we may wonder why this has been put to us as a solemn charge. We should hardly need a basic Commandment to tell us the harmony of life depends on our effort to understand and respect those who brought us into existence.

Yet, as we are looking at the Commandments with open eyes, we may wonder why, even in the days of Moses, it was felt necessary to command Jewish children to respect their fathers and mothers. The command must have been put there because people had been faulty on these points. The Israelites had been tempted by the fleshpots of Egypt. In those times, too, there must have been a severe generation gap and a spirit of alienation, a desire to somehow break out from the slavery imposed on the Israelites. Then, as now, the Commandment emphasized what was natural. We may even think about it in modern psychoanalytic terms.

Freud sought to understand the ills of man through the basic relationship to mother and father, from infancy; he has shown us how deep, instinctual drives can create a hostility toward one parent or the other. If these problems are so deep in us, perhaps they deserve the emphasis of a Commandment. Perhaps our ancient tribal ways were based on such an intuition.

The social laws

The last five Commandments are very clearly a single group, the heading for a code of social laws. Here, there is simple universality. Do we need these admonitions as Commandments? More than ever, it would seem.

Men have discovered methods of mass

The dread mushroom cloud of the atomic bomb, symbol of man's power to destroy. Amid its din a "still small voice" still says, "Thou shalt not murder."

murder that were unknown in the time of Moses. As to adultery, it often leads to murder. Today, with various medical discoveries that have reduced the fear of disease and the fear of accidental pregnancies, the profound bond between a man and a woman who have decided to make their life together is more easily disrupted than ever before. Adultery is of course a form of stealing, stealing someone else's partner, stealing love from one's own partner, and just as murder and adultery and theft are linked, so is falsity. And linked to all these, indeed, in a way, the cause of all such troubles, is to covet. To want what is someone else's, his wife, his house, his fields, or in the days of Moses, his male or female slave, his ox, his ass, or in our own days, his car, his position, his honors. Such jealousy and lust can drive us to bring false charges, to gossip, to connive, to steal, to commit adultery, to murder.

Just as the first three Commandments form a unit related to God, so the last five form a unit related to human society. It is this last unit that most people clearly recall, and that they will start with if you ask them to recite the Ten Commandments.

No one can claim we no longer have need for them. Few people live out their lives without breaking one or more of the Commandments. That is why we need them so constantly before us, as much today as ever, though we may read them a little differently than when they came down from Sinai. They seemed forever fixed, unchangeable— their very brevity has made them eternally fresh and provocative. It is part of Jewish wisdom, part of Judaism, that they be constantly examined, interpreted, renewed.

18   If for myself alone am I, what am I?

If I am not for me
Who will be?
If for myself alone am I
What am I?
And if not now,
Then when,
Then when?

A rhyme, a riddle, a philosophy, this verse was stamped onto the earth of Galilee by the bare feet of the pioneers, the ḥalutzim who came early in our century to reclaim the land. They were called "the barefoots," since they usually had no shoes. But they had ardor. After laboring all day, they would dance the *hora* far into the night. But the odd thing is that the favorite hora tune of these young people, students who wanted to be barefoot laborers, godless socialists, who had returned to the Holy Land, was really a verse from the *Pirke Avot*, the Sayings of the Fathers. It was a saying of the wise, profound, pithy and wittiest of early Rabbis, Hillel himself.

Around and around they would pound, shouting the words until they were hoarse, until only the key words came, in a breathless gasp, "Me . . . be . . . what . . . I" and over and over, echoing into the hills, the

152

Hebrew cry that seemed to pierce beyond the night and the sky, *émantai? émantai?* "If not now then when?"

Seeking the answers

The rhyme was the essence of Jewish social philosophy. It was what we had already known in the time of Hillel and what we had lost and learned again through all the centuries that intervened. How much for ourselves? How much for others? Can it even be right to give up our own selves, entirely, for the sake of others?

When we first perceive that our parents had the same doubts and problems that come to us, and that they never entirely solved them, we either love our parents all the more because of this, or if we are still childish, we feel angry that they failed to provide all the answers for us. But as we mature we will sensibly inquire how much we can learn from the answers partially found by our parents, and by our past generations of parents. In a very Jewish way, Rabbi Hillel took the central questions of social existence and made us feel the answers in the way he put the questions. And with a sighing touch of humor he left the problem to each person to adjust for himself.

Respecting ourselves

To help us we already have the Ten Commandments, and the Golden Rule pointed out by the same Rabbi Hillel, as the sum of

Not for themselves alone, but for themselves and others! Hapoel Hatzair dancers express their joy and enthusiasm in an Israeli folk dance. Hapoel Hatzair of "The Young Workers" was the first labor party established in Palestine.

all our morality; the rule, whether it is put frontwards or backwards, as "do" or "don't," tells us to equate our feelings for our neighbors with our feelings for ourselves. "Love thy neighbor as thyself," says the Torah, but what if we don't love ourselves?

There are people who consciously or unconsciously despise themselves. They hate the way they look. They hate their lack of self-confidence. They hate their place in life. And unfortunately they seem to follow the great rule by having the same lack of love for other people as they have for themselves.

There are Jews who hate themselves for being Jews. If we are to judge by stories about American Jews in what is called our self-hating literature, this is a very widespread sickness.

To such people, of course, the first part of Hillel's profound rhyme is the most needed. "If I am not for me, who will be?"

Hillel was reminding us of what is perhaps a missing commandment, "Thou shalt respect thyself." It may be induced as a part of the commandment to honor, to respect, your mother and father, but perhaps it needed special emphasis. If we believe, as Judaism teaches, in the worth and beauty of Creation, in ourselves as part of that immeasurable act, then self-respect, and the need to live in such a way that we can feel self-respect, is a divine command.

But does "I" mean only the person in your skin? Today we say identity for "I," and your identity takes in your life with your family, your life with the Jewish people, all the way back into history. Self-respect is imbedded in respect for your people. One would hardly need to underline this, were

it not for the unique work of destruction that has been carried on through the centuries, by anti-Semites, against Jewish self-respect. When the ḥalutzim danced it into the ground with their bare feet against the bare earth, they were emphasizing a truth they had learned very directly, in their own lives, in the face of pogroms. Today the truth may seem self-evident and therefore we may more easily forget it, as we shall see.

In Israel, the sons of the ḥalutzim were given no chance to forget Hillel's first line. "If I am not for me," the Jews of Israel asked themselves, "who will be?" For in the world, recognition of their right to life came only when they fought for themselves.

Caring about others

But the second line of Hillel's axiom comes on strongly, as though to erase any trace of selfishness in the first. "If I am for myself alone, what am I?"

Nothing. A clod of earth.

Again we are confronted with two impulses, selfishness and unselfishness in their extremes, feeding back and forth into each other. By these two interacting impulses, Judaism guides us. They may at times seem destructive of each other, but when we succeed in uniting them, our mission as Jews is being fulfilled.

Let us take a simple example first. In almost every great city there is a Jewish hospital, perhaps originally established for reasons of kashrut or because Jews were keeping an old tradition not to burden the non-Jewish community. In modern times, such hospitals, although basically supported by Jews, are of course open to all, and Jews may well be a minority among the patients. Often the name of the hospital will be Sinai, as though to remind us of our ethical commitment. Some of the greatest advances in medical research, benefiting all mankind, have been carried out in these Jewish-endowed hospitals, which usually have the highest reputation for excellence as training centers. In this simple way, what we originally had to do for ourselves now serves the general community. "If I am for myself alone, what am I?"

The code of social concern that has been part of Jewish community life from the beginning has spread beyond any tribal border. According to O. S. Rankin, in *Israel's Wisdom Literature,* the rule to "Love thy neighbor as thyself" was originally intended for the actual neighbor, living in the same area —a "good neighbor" policy. But the rule has long been universalized, and to such a degree that we sometimes have to be reminded that it does not mean "Love thy neighbor before thyself," or even "Love thy neighbor against thyself."

Keeping our balance

In some circles, particulary amongst idealistic young radicals, Jews have to be reminded that we still have life-and-death problems of our own people, so eager are they to show themselves that we are not "for ourselves alone." Today when a Jewish college student takes a special interest in Judaism, some of his radical Jewish friends,

Concerned young people holding a Vietnam memorial service in the UAHC Chapel.

more interested in Maoism or Buddhism, may accuse him of being "for himself alone," or "narrow," or "chauvinistic," the worst word of all!

There is only good to be found in objectively studying other traditions, other approaches to life. Sometimes it is advisable to do so, not only to understand their aims but also to be alert to their possible dangers, limits, or misrepresentations. But we should give ourselves the benefit of first knowing our own. The Hillel rhyme puts the self first, and not out of selfishness, but because until we have a self we cannot deal with others, we cannot judge their needs, and may only harm them as well as ourselves if we try.

The Jew by his long tradition knows that the well-being of others is part of his own life. His religion makes charity the highest duty, the highest virtue. We see this in such tales as that of the rabbi, on his way to the most solemn services of the year, Yom Kippur's *Kol Nidre,* who failed to reach the *shul* until the service was completed because he stopped on the way at the hut of a poor, sick Jew, found the fire out, and stayed to chop wood for him.

Care of the widow, care of the aged, care of the sick, education for the poor, all these things that are now part of the "welfare state" were through the ages part of Jewish community life. With emancipation from the ghetto, Jews quickly applied their own community duties to the community at large. Wealthy Jews in America established foundations which were the first to help Negroes fight for their civil rights. And this was not altogether unselfish. The principle of the fight against racial discrimination meant safeguarding Jewish rights together with those of Negroes and all others.

Remembering our base

But no man, in his care for others, should despise himself, and the danger of this comes, again and again, in highly idealistic movements. There came a time when Negroes, in their own fight for full equality, used anti-Semitic slogans, even against Jewish schoolteachers. Some young Jews who considered themselves leftists tended to go right along with this attitude. If being for the Negro meant swallowing some of the extreme racist Negro statements against Jews—picked up even from Nazi slogans— then it was "temporarily necessary."

People can be led to such inside-out behavior when they have lost their base. Judaism, with beautiful simplicity, provides that base in such a balanced proposition as Hillel's rhyme. One must be for oneself but not for oneself alone. One must preserve one's identity but one is obliged to help all the oppressed, all the needy, through universal concern. What should have been done in that specific situation? That which many concerned people—not Jews alone—undertook to do. They exposed to the Negroes themselves the dangerous sources of their slogans, they helped concentrate on the real causes and the remedies for the Negro situation, in the schools and elsewhere. To some extent the situation was helped. But it is one to which we must be constantly alert, for unhappily there is a long history in which people, especially Jews, are needlessly asked to destroy their own identity for the sake of "universal good," or "world revolution." Our most idealistic young Jews are often led into this, as though the advance of humanity could not take place without Jews ceasing to be Jews!

Lessons from disappointments

The pattern may be seen in the early revolutionary movements in Russia. As usual, warmhearted, idealistic young Jewish intellectuals were the first to flock to the movement. The slogans of Marxism awakened the messianic mission in us. An early disappointment came when the revolutionists refused to pass a resolution condemning the Kishinev pogrom of 1903. But still, brilliant young Jews, like Trotsky, gave their lives to the movement. Then when socialist Jews tried to carry their ideals to Palestine, the "revolution" became and remained anti-Zionist —later, anti-Israel. Long after the revolution had triumphed in Russia, its proponents continued to suppress Jewish identity and culture, not to speak of religion, since all religions were attacked. At the point where this campaign to erase a people's sense of itself, as regard the Jews, had virtually succeeded, Communists in other countries began to see that the idea might in the long run be applied to them, too. The Hungarians, and then the Czechs, found their national life being encroached upon by force of arms. Their freedom was under attack, and being

eroded. Further, individual rights of choice and freedom of creative literary expression were curtailed for non-Jewish citizens also under totalitarian regimes.

Where, then, was the professed higher ideal of "the movement"? Yet despite this long lesson, the intellectuals and radicals of the American New Left, many Jewish, could be deluded by the same mistaken idealism, and could accept an anti-Israel position in their politics. And this, at a time when the Jews of Israel were openly marked for genocide by their Arab enemies. Plainly, the first part of Hillel's axiom is as fundamental as the second. "If I am not for me, who will be?" is as basic to the Jew as "If for myself alone am I, what am I?"

Confrontation—now

The rhyme goes on to ask, "If not now, then when? When?" This is not a passive question. It is a demand. It becomes a command. And it is not an old saw, an easy proverb against procrastination, such as "Don't put off until tomorrow what you can do today." It is a continuous, always immediate confrontation with the world's fate.

The world is today, now. The world of man is an ever-changing moment. Judaism teaches that the development of humanity is all in one with God's act of creation, continuously taking place. This is what we speak of as God revealing Himself in history. History is in movement toward the messianic ideal, to be reached through the working-out of the forces of good and evil, into the ultimate good.

"If not now, then when?" really means there is no "when." The Jewish command means that what is put off has lost its place in the proper sequence of things, in the ultimate harmony of the universe. Therefore alertness and action are required of us. All those who cry out for an activist creed already have it in Hillel's code.

The Jew is not centered on the afterlife; while the question is left open, his sense of immortality is imbedded in the never-ending effect of our good actions, on earth, as they become part of the eternal stream of life. This is eloquently pointed out by the first Jew to become a member of the Supreme Court, Louis D. Brandeis, for whom Brandeis University is named. In an essay called "Our Richest Inheritance," in 1915, he said, "Nearly every other people has reconciled their world of suffering with the idea of a beneficent providence by conceiving of immortality for the individual." But we Jews do not shape our actions around that idea of heaven. Heaven and hell are used as illustrations, hardly more.

Another great Jewish thinker, Ahad Ha-Am, quoted by Brandeis, said:

Judaism did not turn heavenward and create in Heaven an eternal habitation of souls. It found eternal life on earth by strengthening the social feeling in the individual, by making him regard himself not as an isolated being, with an existence bounded by birth and death, but as part of a larger whole, as a limb of a social body. This conception shifts the center of gravity not from the flesh to the spirit, but from the individual to the community . . . with this shifting the problem of life becomes not a problem of the individual, but of social life. I live for the sake of the perpetuation and happiness of the community of which I am a member: I die to make room for new individuals who will mold the community afresh and not allow it to stagnate and remain forever in one position. When the individual thus values the community as his own life, and strives after its happiness as though it were his individual well-being, he finds satisfaction, and no longer feels so keenly the bitterness of his individual existence, because he sees the end for which he suffers.

"This," says Brandeis, "is our inheritance, such is the estate which we hold in trust. And what are the terms of the trust; what the obligations imposed? The short answer is: *noblesse oblige.*"

Jewish experience

Perhaps, avoiding claim to spiritual nobility, we should rather say, "Experience teaches us." We have been through slavery, we have been through the worst kinds of discrimination, and we are obliged by this experience to teach and to help those who still suffer from such wrongs.

That is why our scholars and teachers are constantly looking back into our experience and into our writings to find their deepest meanings. When we first read a work of literature, as children, we may grasp the story and find it wonderful, but when we reread the same work as we grow up, we find new understanding. The same is true of the Jewish people and our Scriptures.

We have already mentioned that far back in our tribal days, the word *neighbor* was probably understood to mean the nearby tribe, with whom feuds might occur. Yet Rabbi Leo Baeck interprets this differently. "According to the Bible, everyone is 'our' brother and 'our' neighbor," he wrote.

Not only every member of our family, our tribe and our people, but every man is our brother. Neither affection nor good will make him "our brother"; no social institutions nor national constitution grants him this status. It is through God that every man is our fellow man. That is why the Bible speaks of "thy brother . . . be he a stranger or sojourner" (Lev. 25:35). The poor man who comes before you is "thy poor" (Ex. 23:6) and "thy needy" (Deut. 15:11) just as the stranger who abides with you is "thy stranger" (Ex. 20:10). We are all related to each other by God since "the Lord is the maker of us all" (Prov. 22:2).

The Passover call

The call that we make at the Passover Seder, the call that was first made just after we ourselves had escaped from four hundred years of slavery, is a universal cry to the whole world, "Let all who are hungry come and eat, let all who are needy come and be satisfied."

We do not believe that one man suffered for the sins of the whole world, nor that one nation suffers for the sins of all other nations. Judaism implies a belief in actively seeking out all the causes of suffering, and doing what can be done, now, to alleviate suffering, to make everyone's life more noble. But not, in that process, to demean or destroy our own. That, indeed, would be against God.

The sharing of Seder embraces all. At the head of this table a white-garbed newcomer to Israel conducts the Seder in a JDC Malben home for the aged. Contemporaries from many lands live here.

19 How can one still believe, in such a troubled world?

With the end of the Second World War, as stories came out about what had happened in Auschwitz and other death camps, there came a touching and awesome report that a song rose up from the long lines of Jews going to their death in the gas chambers, and that this song was *Ani Ma-amin*, "I Believe."

> *I believe with perfect faith*
> *In the coming of Messiah;*
> *And though he tarry*
> *Nevertheless, I do believe.*

The words are from the creed of Maimonides; they form the last of the Thirteen Points he wrote down as essential to Judaism. It is not unusual, as we have seen, for the words of a philosopher to be turned into a Jewish song. Our deepest expressions of belief have a way of turning into music, music from the very heart. The philosophy of Hillel became a song of life for the early pioneers in Israel, and so the words of another Jewish philosopher, we are told, were chanted in the face of death in Europe.

Were they, really? Could it have been possible for the masses of Jews, coming out of the horror transports, the boxcars in which they had been packed and dragged for days and nights on their way to the death camps, then moving along the "selection" line in which families were torn apart, with those who looked strong enough being sent into the labor line, and the rest into the extermination line—could it still have been possible for the doomed to sing? and to sing a religious song?

Faith in adversity

We do not really know. Survivors who have described the death camps do not dwell on such incidents. It would be romantic to say that, day and night, they heard the words of "I Believe" rising with the smoke of the holocaust.

Survivors have given us many books and accounts of this program which went on, winter and summer, over a period of three years in the final, specially built gas-chamber camps, and which seemed to defy every imagined limit to the urge for evil. In many of these accounts there will appear the figure of the saintly personality, the pious Jew, sometimes a rabbi, who despite the worst conditions of the camp continued with his worship, and found ways to help those who suffered most painfully. We are again and again given descriptions of how small groups of pious Jews would gather in a corner on a Sabbath and on High Holidays to repeat the prayers, and of how, in these starvation camps, there were still those who neverthe-less abstained from eating even their starva-tion ration on the Day of Atonement. In a few cases, we are told of Jews who managed to smuggle their *Tefillin* into the camp itself,

and continued to say their daily prayers right to the end. And so, in some instances, the song of Messiah must have been sung even in the death chamber.

Messianic prophecies

But more meaningful for us is the part of the story that we ourselves have seen to be true, the fact that the whole world seized on this awesome image and accepted it as the symbol of the holocaust. We all want, we all need, to believe that despite the very worst that man can do, the good impulse remains in the face of evil, and that men retain their faith that messianic times will surely come.

Again, this is a concept that arose in Ju-daism, that has been adopted outside of Judaism as well, that indeed became the center of Christianity, and that Jews them-selves interpret in differing ways. Joseph Klausner wrote that the messianic hope is the Jew's gift to the world. The Jews could give birth to such a belief because they found themselves again and again in need of deliverance. The Talmud describes Moses as the first deliverer, the Messiah as the last.

But our recorded prophecies of the com-ing of messianic times did not begin with Moses in Egypt; they began in another time of oppression, when the defeated Jews were led away from Jerusalem to Babylon. The most vivid of these prophecies is in the words of Ezekiel, who had a vision of the dry bones of the dead filling a valley in Babylonia, and cried out,

Oh ye dry bones, hear the word of the Lord: . . .
Behold, I will cause breath to enter into you,
And ye shall live.

—Ezekiel 37:4-5

This vision of dead bones being animated by God into living men, a vision of resurrection, was interpreted by the prophet to mean the "restoration of the whole house of Israel." At first it was a dream of the nation restored. It harked back to the story of Adam, with God breathing life into man.

But this powerful wish for national revival soon centered on the idea of another leader who would restore the days of wisdom and justice, as in the times of David and Solomon. Thus, Isaiah prophesied, "And there shall come forth a shoot out of the stock of Jesse [the father of David] . . . And the spirit of the Lord shall rest upon him, the spirit of wisdom and understanding, the spirit of counsel and might." The days of peace would come when "the wolf shall dwell with the lamb," and the Lord would "gather up the scattered of Judah from the four corners of the earth." Swords would be beaten into plowshares, and nations would learn war no more. (Isa. 11:1, 2, 6, 12; 2:4)

Legends of the Tishbite

Supernatural legends about the coming of a Messiah grew up around the striking figure of the prophet Elijah, who had miraculously been carried up to heaven in a fiery chariot drawn by horses of fire. According to these legends, Elijah would be sent down again, as miraculously as he had been drawn up.

This Elijah cup depicts the "king" riding in humility on a donkey (Zechariah 9:9). It was engraved in Russia in the eighteenth century.

He would be sent down to help his people in their worst times of distress.

Through the centuries, these legends grew. Elijah, seeing the suffering of the Jews on earth, would plead in heaven for the Messiah to be sent down, even before his appointed time. Thus, we have the haunting folksong of Elijah.

Eliyahu of Prophecy,
Eliyahu the Tishbi,
Eliyahu the Giladi,
Come unto us
In our own day
With Messiah ben David.

Hopes and disappointments

Though the messianic idea was one of national rescue, there was already in it, from earliest times, the idea of universal peace. Out of Jerusalem the word would go forth, said the prophets. Presently the Jews were permitted to return to Jerusalem, and they built their Temple for the second time, but they were still subjects of a foreign ruler. The Jews recovered their independence with the Maccabees, but the warring nations conquered them again, and as their troubles deepened, the only way out, more than ever, seemed to be through the appearance of the Messiah. Some saw him in Jesus, some saw him in Bar Kokhba, yet with each disappointment the faith did not die. In scores of passages in the Talmud we learn of the Messiah. The idea developed that the sending of Messiah was part of the Creator's plan at the very inception of the universe. "From

the beginning of Creation, King Messiah was born, for he entered the mind of God even before the world was created."

Thus, in times as troubled as our own, Judaism did not turn away from the world to the idea of eternal peace in heaven, but still insisted that life on earth was part of the vast purpose of creation. A divine concept was in progress. All history is part of it, and we can survive Auschwitz because that too is only a part of the process, which comes to fruition in what we call messianic times.

Though this vision already existed when the Talmud was being compiled, the messianic idea was still seen in a human image —just as for a long time people could not conceive of God except in a human, anthropomorphic image. And so people kept asking, "Who will be the Messiah?" In every age, the Jews cried out, "Things are so bad, surely the Messiah has come down among us. Who can the Messiah be?" In Rome, in 1522, there appeared a splendid person who called himself Prince Reubeni, and claimed to be a brother of a Jewish king, descendant of the Ten Lost Tribes, who ruled somewhere in the East. Instantly, Prince Reubeni aroused the hopes of masses of Jews who were ready to follow him to Jerusalem.

In Portugal, in the same period, when the Inquisition was still highly active, there appeared from among the secret Jews, the Marranos, a young man named Solomon Molcho, who went to Rome; he prophesied the overflow of the Tiber, which indeed took place in 1530, and an earthquake in Lisbon, which happened in 1531. Prince Reuveni now took the role of Elijah, while Shlomo Molcho was taken up as a Messiah, thus they could be the necessary twain. Molcho was eventually executed. Reuveni also lost his life in the course of the persecutions.

A century later, at a time of widespread pogroms, there appeared Shabbetai Zvi of Smyrna, Turkey, a Kabbalist who proclaimed the ineffable Name in the synagogue, and declared that he was the Messiah. All over Eastern Europe, where the Chmielnicki massacres had broken out, Jews packed their belongings and made ready for deliverance. Shabbetai Zvi visited Jerusalem, and returned to stir up even greater numbers of followers. He declared 1648 the year of salvation and sailed for Constantinople, since the Holy Land was then ruled by the Turks. He intended to have the Sultan restore Israel to the Jews. Instead, the Sultan imprisoned him. Given the choice of death or conversion, Shabbetai accepted the Moslem faith.

Growth of Zionism

In the time of Theodor Herzl, many Jews insisted that he must be the Messiah, though he was of course opposed to any such pretensions. On the other hand, there were religious Jews who rejected Zionism because, they said, the return to Jerusalem could only take place when the Messiah appeared in person.

This too was a period of widespread pogroms. But as the Zionist movement grew, and attracted nonreligious Jews, the idea of Messiah began to be interpreted in a more general way. It was seen less as a personal than as a spiritual conception—if one may use the word "spiritual" for the nonreligious. Together with the ideal of a revived Jewish land, there were powerful social ideals. It began to appear as though the people themselves were acting on the messianic impulse implanted in mankind.

Messianism as a world mission

The Jewish idea, from long ago, of the Messiah as an instrument of national revival, of the restoration of Jerusalem, seemed to be carried out by the Zionist movement. The broader messianic idea, both Christian and Jewish, of Messiah as a symbol of universal justice was being advanced by world socialist movements. Despite all human evil, messianism was seen as the mission of mankind.

Again, this is expressed by Rabbi Leo Baeck. In *The Essence of Judaism*, he speaks of the messianic element as a commandment.

"The commandment is infinite," he says, for "a task which can be concluded is not really a task." The task which man sets for himself, "the petty everyday things, he can attain in his life, but the tasks which God sets him are beyond his earthly existence. . . ."

While no individual can do so, mankind itself may look forward to the complete realization of the good. Mankind will attain man's mission. . . . Mankind is seen as extending in all time, just as it extends all over the earth. It thus signifies not only the unity of nations, each a part of the whole of mankind, but also the unity of the days in which each generation is a part of history, a step forward along the path at the end of which stands fulfillment. The unity of the nations and the unity of the ages—the two together constitute man's world. One century follows and gives birth to another, all of them issuing from the creation and leading to the fulfillment.

. . . Each individual existence is thereby enabled to reach beyond itself and into the ages; it becomes part of the flow of all human existence.

Therefore the evil that we see in wars, hunger, unconcern, all this is not the end of man. We were among the first to hope, and have survived. As Milton Steinberg reminds us—

Beyond the sphere of Judaism, men of antiquity had no hopes for the future. They expected at best that what had been would be forevermore, if indeed they were not persuaded that the world was running steadily downhill from a Golden Age distant in the past . . . It was a great revolution which Judaism affected with its good tiding of a Kingdom, a turning forward of the eyes, upward of the heart, onward of the feet; in sum, a reorientation of the total human being.

The revolution was all the greater because, with time, it overflowed all churches and all creeds, to become the common property and inspiration of all men of good will, whether devout or irreligious.

The years of waiting

Then why does it take so long to bring the time of Messiah? A poet has described the Jewish folk conception, out of our legends, of a kind of divine desire to give us Messiah, and yet of the impossibility of hastening the divine process. Heinrich Heine wrote this in his story of a visit with the great Rabbi Manasseh ben Naphtali in Cracow, who told him a Talmudic tale:

The Messiah, he said, was born on the day when Jerusalem was destroyed by the villains, Titus and Vespasian, and ever since he has been living in the most beautiful palace in Heaven, surrounded by brightness and joy, wearing a crown upon his head, just like a king—but his hands are fettered by golden chains.

"What is the meaning of these golden chains?" I asked in amazement. "They are necessary," replied the great Rabbi with a wise look and deep sigh. "Without these fetters the Messiah, losing patience, might suddenly plunge down and start his work of deliverance too early, at the wrong time. He is no quiet sleepyhead. He is a handsome, very slender, but immensely strong man, thriving like youth itself; and he leads a very monotonous life. He spends the best part of the morning with the customary prayers, or laughing and joking with his servants, angels in disguise, who sing prettily and play the flute. Then he has his long hair combed, and is anointed with nard and dressed in his princely purple. All afternoon he studies the Cabbala. Towards evening he sends for his old chancellor, another angel in disguise, as are the four strong councillors who accompany him. Then the chancellor must read to his master, from a large book, what has happened all day. There are all sorts of stories at which the Messiah smiles with pleasure, or shakes his head in disapproval. But when he hears how his people are abused below, he gets most fearfully angry and cries out so that the heavens tremble —then the four strong councillors must hold back the enraged one lest he rush down to earth, and they truly would fail to overpower him if his hands were not fettered with the golden chains. In the end they soothe him, with gentle reminders that the time, the true hour of salvation, is yet to come, and he sinks down to his couch and veils his face and weeps. . . ."

This was about what Manasseh ben Naphtali told me in Cracow, referring to the Talmud in witness of his credibility. I often had to think of his tale, especially in the most recent times, after the July Revolution. On the worst days I even thought I heard with my own ears the rattling as of golden chains, and then a desperate sobbing . . .

Do not lose heart, beautiful Messiah, you will save not only Israel, but all suffering humanity. Break not your golden chains! . . . Keep him fettered yet a little time, lest he come too soon, the redeeming King of the World.

Too soon? Doubtless because the development of man is unfinished.

We believe

Today again, only our poetic, spiritual belief can sustain us in the face of man's horrors. We can continue to believe, because we nevertheless see the possibilities in mankind, demonstrated all through history. We see that man has gradually accepted his responsibility, has taken the burden of the Messiah to himself, and is striving to redeem himself. If we cherish the unbearably tragic image of those doomed Jews who could sing of their faith in Messiah as they walked to the gas chamber, it is because we inwardly need to hear their song, their appeal. We can continue to have faith in this troubled world only if we accept and assume the command to correct it, to redeem it, and thus to bring us nearer to messianic times.

Heinrich Heine, poet and journalist. After the failure of the 1848 revolution he continued his life work in Paris.

20 Is there life after death?

What, as Jews, do we believe about life after death? Does Judaism teach that we shall live again, on earth? Not necessarily. It is clear that Ezekiel's vision of the valley of dry bones as a symbol of new life is taken to mean that the Jews as a people would rise up to live again.

There is another story which shows that Jews in the time of the Temple were divided on the idea of resurrection. This is the story of Jesus. He is supposed to have risen from his burial cave and to have appeared to a number of persons; the story of his resurrection became part of what a Christian is required to believe. Since the first Christians were Jews who continued to be Jews, it is clear that the vision of a dead man coming to life again was not entirely rejected among the Jews of that day. Tales of magic healing and of the raising of the dead abounded among the populace. Some believed, some did not.

Ideas of Heaven and Hell

But there was another type of idea about life after death, over which the Temple priests, and the Rabbis, were having a profound argument. This was not the idea of resurrection on earth, but of the continuation of some kind of life beyond the earth. Life after death was pictured either as reward in heaven or punishment in hell. Heaven was pictured as a Garden of Eden, and the picture of hell was also taken from a place on earth, indeed it was quite close at hand, the gulley called *Gai Hinnom*, just outside the sheer drop of the Temple walls. There, in ancient days, it was said, the heathen had burned their human sacrifices to Moloch, and so to this place of evil went the evil souls, and *Gai Hinnom* became the word *Gehenna*.

Sadducees and Pharisees

But was this picture of heaven and hell, of reward and punishment, firmly a part of Judaism? Some Rabbis said yes. The priests said no.

The priests were mostly from the aristocratic families, forming the party of the Sadducees, or *Zadokim*—descendants from the family of Zadok, the High Priest. Their Judaism was the Judaism of authority, and the basic authority was the Law of Moses. Everything beyond the Five Books of Moses was of a different nature. It was prophecy, it was poetry, it was history, but it did not have, to them, the binding force of the Law.

And there was nothing in the Law about afterlife. There was nothing about rewards in heaven or punishment in hell. Some Jews believed this left the question open, but the Sadducees believed this closed the whole matter. We have the same style of argument

". . . and ye shall live." The resurrection vision of Ezekiel is shown in fresco on the walls of the synagogue at Dura-Europos (third century c.e.).

today, between people we call *fundamental-
ists*, who say, "Show me where it says so
in the Bible," and others who declare that
everything in the Bible is open to interpretation, and that the absence of a subject from
the Bible leaves us free to make up our
minds on that subject, guided of course, by
the wisdom of our tradition, and all the
knowledge man has pierced to, in nature.

Now, largely because we live in a generally Christian environment, the comparison
of "Pharisees and Sadducees" has been
given a special tone. Another phrase,
"Scribes and Pharisees" has been made to
sound evil. But the word *Pharisee* was a
general term for the scholars and scribes
who developed their ideas about Judaism
from the time the Temple was first destroyed,
when the Jews were taken to captivity in
Babylonia. There, as we know, they established academies, and there the scribes wrote
down the laws, for common discussion.
Babylon continued to be a great center for
Jewish scholarship, even after a large part
of the Jewish population returned to Jerusalem to build the Second Temple. But two
ways of interpretation could now be seen.
The renewal of the priestly services, and the
reign of the king-priests in the time of the
Maccabees, meant authority. But the populace was constantly questioning, puzzling,
imagining, arguing; their scribes and teachers led these explorations; they became
"separate" and the word for separation gave
them their name, the Pharisees. Their view
was broader than that of the king-priests.
They wanted to give weight to what we
would now call the Common Law, the rulings and ideas that were accepted through
common use and belief.

Now, the population rather believed in an
afterlife. Some pictured it as an afterlife of
the spirit, the soul, and some pictured it as
an actual heavenly place where saintly
men were assigned their places in a divine
academy of the Torah.

A belief in the continuation of the spirit
is common in virtually all cultures, and
while the Jews might have picked up some
of their images of heaven and hell from the
Egyptians or from the Persians among whom
they had lived, or from the Greeks who had
invaded them, naturally in the course of
time they had molded these ideas to their
own ethos. By tracing this process in its
main lines, we can, as individuals, decide
what we ourselves believe, for much of this
is optional to us. As with the face of God,
Judaism has the reverence to make no absolute declaration on what is unknowable.

Sayings of the Talmud

Although the question of a world to come
was one of the great conflicts between the
Sadducees and the Pharisees, a few centuries
after the destruction of the Second Temple
the Sadducee point of view had faded. The
Talmud, which then came into being, accepts as a matter of course hundreds of sayings about the world to come, although the
idea of heaven is much more prominent than
the idea of Gehenna. One view is that only
the worthy, the good, have an afterlife, while
the unworthy simply do not attain heaven.

They are left truly dead. However there are also sayings which place the wicked in an afterlife of punishment.

One Talmudic story shows that the argument about an afterlife was still going on, for it tells how a certain Rabbi Yosé ben Ḥalafta tried to convince someone who doubted it. The Rabbi and the doubter were visiting a man whose son had just died. As the Rabbi tried to console the father, telling him he would see his son again in the world to come, the doubter objected. "Man is like a clay pot," he said. "Can pieces of potsherd be mended? Is it not written, 'Thou shalt dash them to pieces like a potter's vessel?'" But the Rabbi said, "What about a vessel made of glass, which can be heated again, and blown? If something which is made by the breath of a human being can be remade, how much more so with that which is made by the breath of the Holy One!"

Modern scholars, such as Isidore Epstein in *Judaism*, have keenly speculated as to whether the Talmud simply restored to Judaism certain beliefs in an afterlife that had been purposely left out of the Torah of Moses. The early Scriptures found it necessary to cast a veil over the whole question of survival beyond the grave, he said, in order to wean people away from the idolatrous cult of the dead with which they had had strong contact in Egypt.

Emphasis on this world

Judaism, less than other religions, indulges in moral balance—the more misery in this world, the greater pleasure in the next. The emphasis is on life on earth. A well-known Talmudic saying is, "Better is one hour of repentance and good deeds in this world than the whole life of the world to come."

Another comment, by Rabbi Jonathan, reminds us that our prophets dwell on what will happen in the days of Messiah, in the ideal future state here on earth. "But as for the world beyond the grave, no eye hath seen, and no ear hath heard, but God alone knows what He hath prepared for those who wait for Him!" This view is echoed by Maimonides, who said that to guide our acts because we expect reward in heaven is "to act like a schoolboy who expects nuts and confections as compensation for his studies."

Parables and folklore

This leaves the image of heaven to the creators of parables, and to folk legends. Some of the most beautiful are in praise of the simple, unassuming, but pure soul. Many of these pointed folk tales are around the question of who will sit next to whom in paradise. Thus, Rabbi Joshua, a highly learned and esteemed person, hears a voice in a dream telling him that his neighbor in paradise will be Nones the Butcher, and that their reward will be the same.

"Woe is me!" cries the learned Rabbi Joshua on awakening. "I have studied the Torah without end, and illuminated the minds of eighty disciples. Now see my reward! It seems I am no better than Nones the Butcher, whoever he may be!" In one town after another, Rabbi Joshua searches for this butcher. At last he finds his future companion, and questions him. It turns out that the butcher has a father and mother who are old and ill. He tells his visitor, "I have given up all pleasures, and attend to their needs. I wash them and dress them and prepare their food with my own hands." Whereupon Rabbi Joshua declares, "How happy I am to have the distinction of being your companion in paradise!"

A thousand years later, in Kabbalism and Ḥasidism, we encounter another form of popular belief in life after death, and this is the form of rebirth on earth, called *gilgul*. The soul is sent back into another body. Here, Jewish folklore at times shares with other cultures the idea of reincarnation, even in an animal form, to expiate wrongdoing.

This drowsy little boy was trying to keep his mind on the letters. In such a household, around 1910, he would grow up into a world rich in parable and folklore, the tradition of Eastern European Jewry.

Harmony of the earthly and heavenly

In *Judaism* Isidore Epstein tells us the earthly and the heavenly are not opposed to each other. On the contrary, "the earthly and the heavenly are in the view of Judaism in harmonious relationship."

This harmony is seen in Judaism's doctrine of man. Although composed of two different elements, the earthly body and the heavenly soul, man is a unity. Judaism rejects the dualistic idea of a pure spirit imprisoned in a body which is impure and hostile to the spiritual and material. For Judaism, body and spirit have been united to one another in order to give rise together to a higher form of earthly life—the righteous man.

The conception of man as co-worker with God, both now and in eternity, gives a new and higher significance to the doctrine of immortality. . . . It is grounded in God and in His purpose in which man is called upon to cooperate. Immortality is thus no longer merely a survival beyond the grave, but the homegoing of the spirit or the soul of man to the further cultivation and development of the divine relationship made manifest on this stage of life.

Eternal life of the people

Professor Salo Baron reminds us that the Jewish idea of immortality is really embodied in the continuation of the people itself, in the part that each soul contributes to a divine idea that is still being revealed. The lack of Biblical reference to the idea of individual life after death is well known, he says.

Both early and later Judaism, however, continuously affirmed belief in the survival of the group and in the "eternal" life of the Jewish people down to, and beyond, the Messianic age . . . What really matters in the Jewish religion is not the immortality of the individual Jew, but that of the Jewish people.

Even when, later, Judaism adapted the belief in the immortality of the soul and physical resurrection, the central point remained the eternal life of the nation. Hence the extraordinary attachment to life manifested by Orthodox Jews. Life on earth, the care of the sick and and the poor, the duty of marriage and increase in family—all these are repeatedly stressed, that the race and the people may be maintained until the end of days.

The idea of immortality

The idea of resurrection is still accepted today by Orthodox Jewry, and by some individual Conservative and Reform adherents. But all three branches of Judaism uphold the idea of immortality.

What is meant by *immortality*? A human being may leave works on earth that are called immortal, traces of his personality may remain and influence future persons, through art, through writing, through inventiveness, through politics. Every person lives on for some time in the memory of those who knew him, and may live on indefinitely through descendants. But we also have a sense of the immortality of the soul. If we believe in the eventual existence of justice, the span of human life may be too short for us to see it come about, yet by and large in our personal lives, those who live out the fullness of their years find that they do see a basic sort of justice taking place. There seems to be time in a full human life for goodness to be recognized, for evil to be punished. Of course this does not always happen. But one cannot say the world is totally unjust.

However, in the larger sense, the span of human life is too brief for most of us to witness that creation is indeed being carried forward to justice. In this, we feel that there must be a spiritual continuation of our being, a life of the soul that may join in some unknowable way, in the timelessness of the beyond, in the eventual enjoyment of divine justice. This is our immortality.

21 The Other

In a sudden flash of clarity we see the answer to a problem. Most often, this comes in mathematics. Sometimes it comes in a kind of half-dream. We see the solution so clearly we are sure we will never lose it. And then, somehow, we lose it. We try to work our way back to the answer, step by step; sometimes we recover it, sometimes it eludes us, and sometimes we think there was nothing ever there. This is akin to certain religious experiences, to the visions of the mystics, and to an entire "other" aspect of Judaism. We might think of it as the far side of revelation.

The elusive vision

Moses had a revelation; though he knew that he might not see the face of God and live, the revealed knowledge of God became clear to him, and he brought back with him the basic answers for an ethical life in a compact between God and man. The Jewish people, mainly, grasped his vision. But again and again it seemed to slip out of their grasp, shimmering and insubstantial. Again and again there came prophets who caught the vision and tried to show it to the rest of the people. And always, as had happened in the very beginning between Moses and the followers of Korah, there were nay-sayers, who could not see. And there have also always been the intensifiers, who saw beyond what most people saw.

Doubting not departure

As a whole our people has tried to work its way to God step by step, while some Jews, at every step, questioned if the vision was mistaken; and that is why Judaism remains an open religion, a knowledge that we have agreed to live by God's ethic, with a continuous quest and questioning into the mystery of God. And that is why there is the "other" side of Judaism, the far side that even Jews themselves sometimes mistake for rejection, disbelief, apostasy. Our folk use their own word, *apikores*, a conglomeration of Yiddish, Hebrew, and Greek, for anyone they imagine has strayed from the faith. It comes from the Greek philosophy of Epicurus, brought to Judea during Greek dominance, a philosophy of refined enjoyment that attracted sophisticated Jerusalemites of that day. So today, among highly observant Jews, *apikores* is used all the way from a humorous epithet to a curse.

In the Yiddish world, still so close to us, an *apikores* might simply be someone who started reading books of science; in the period of Enlightenment this was a common epithet. First an *apikores* read Darwin, then he tasted pork, and he was lost! But in our light, today, that person still might be very

deeply and devoutly a Jew. Reform Jews were called *apikorsim*, and are still called that by the extremely Orthodox. All this is easy enough to understand; it is like a quarrel within the family. But—like bad family quarrels—it can also lead to the extreme end, to departure, if everyone is rigid.

A dangerous fallacy

There is continuous danger of misunderstanding, especially in modern times, with the scientific attitude of doubting everything until it is factually proved. Some people feel that doubt indicates total denial. And often it is our own Jewish intellectuals who mix up the two.

A striking example of this can be found in a book called *The American Jews*, by James Yaffe. The example is an interesting one because it reflects the loose thinking, the sloganized propaganda, that is the danger of the era of easy, widespread communication. The writer offers the example of three outstanding men who have, more than any others, affected modern thinking. All three of them, he says, were Jews, and all three "to a greater or lesser degree," departed from Judaism. The three were Karl Marx, Sigmund Freud, and Albert Einstein.

The example, a rather dangerous one, is repeated here because it is mistaken in the same way as those who lump together all who depart from the strict rules of observance as *apikorsim*. It is precisely this type of assertion, with a grain of truth in it, that may confuse us. Not only James Yaffe has offered this seemingly striking observation; it is one that comes up commonly.

The grain of truth is of course that Marx, Einstein, and Freud were all of Jewish descent and that none practiced formal Judaism. But the whole truth is different. The impression left by such a statement is that since the greatest Jews of modern times departed from Judaism, all intelligent Jews should do the same. The plain fact is, of course, that Karl Marx was born into a converted family, his father having adopted Christianity for career reasons. Marx never discarded Judaism since he was not raised as a Jew. While Einstein and Freud did not go around wearing *yarmulkes*, both were active Jews all their lives, and thought and wrote profoundly on the subject of Judaism. Freud delivered his very first paper on psychoanalysis to his B'nai B'rith club in Vienna; he lived in Jewish circles; his son was a member of a Zionist youth group; and as we shall see, there was a strong connection between psychoanalytic discoveries and mystical Judaism. Einstein, whose views we have already quoted, actually campaigned with Chaim Weizmann in America for the Zionist cause, and was attached to Judaism all his life, though as a scientist he classified the early Mosaic phase as a cult religion. Both of these men were undeniably good Jews, attached to their tradition, even if "doubters." Karl Marx, on the other hand, wrote distorted, vitriolic descriptions of Jews as greedy exploiters. He unfortunately started the Communist movement in an anti-Semitic direction which it has never entirely lost. Here is a sample of his writing:

Sigmund Freud, bringing light to dark recesses of the human mind, introduced the science and practice of psychoanalysis. His theories—with some modifications—are still followed. They have influenced anthropology, literature, education, and the arts.

What is the object of the Jew's worship in this world? Usury. What is his worldly god? Money.

The irony is that the Communist ideal—not to be confused with what has so far happened in actual practice—is itself a form of the messianic idea of a Golden Age, which came from Judaism. If a practicing American Jewish writer today can put Marx, Einstein, and Freud into the same classification as to their Jewishness, it is not enough merely to call this a fallacy; we must look more deeply into the causes of such assumptions.

Self-criticism not self-destruction

There is a difference between self-criticism and self-destruction. Jewish tradition has always given room to self-criticism. What were the prophets but critics of the community? As well as critics, we had doubters, and such a one appears in a stirring novel about Bar Kokhba, *The Son of a Star*, by Theodore Meisels. In this vivid book about the last great Jewish revolt against the Romans, there is a character named *Aḥer*—the Other. This is the name given by the Jews of his time to an unbeliever, whose real name they even refuse to utter. [He was Elisha ben Avuyah.] *Aḥer* is not an *apikores*; he had been a brilliant student in the academy of Rabbi Akiva, but he had one day simply lost his belief in God. The devout circle around the great Rabbi then called him the Other, but they did not send him away. Though they bitterly reviled him, though they were angry at his attempts to mislead students from the study of the Torah, he remained. This is, in a painful degree, the faithful unfaithful, the questioner, the seeker who, when he cannot find God, may declare he has lost all belief. Still, he remains within the Jewish fold, for the community somehow understands what is troubling him. It is what to a lesser degree troubles us all. It is the desperate inner desire for a complete answer, the desire to go beyond the limitations of man.

The rational approach

This desire may drive us in either of two directions. One is the rational. It is the way of Maimonides, of Spinoza, of Einstein. It is the attempt to learn more about the rules of the universe, about the way in which God has carried out creation, even though we are aware that the final truth, the First Cause, the Fiftieth Door, is closed to us. The rational approach may seek a naturalistic explanation for the dividing of the sea to let the Israelites pass, or for the fire that came down on the altar of Elijah, it may include an anthropological explanation for the tribal rules in the books of Moses. It may, in modern times, include socialist Zionists who believe that the people themselves will be Messiah. But we have gone far past the point of view that suspected every scientist of being antireligious, every socialist of being an atheist. We know that in the larger sense these people are within the Jewish faith.

Baruch Spinoza, seventeenth-century advocate of free thought, is regarded as the father of modern Biblical criticism, and indeed of modern philosophy.

The mystical approach

The second direction of exploration, also within the body of Judaism, and indeed some believe close to the very heart of it, is the other side of the rational—it is the mystical. To connect a great scientist like Freud to the mystical side of Jewish belief may seem wild, but we already know, as Freud himself has shown us, how each impulse in life contains its opposite. Freud opened a field of science that some scholars still declare is not a science because the scientific method of controlled experimental testing does not suit it. Freud's discoveries in psychoanalysis are based sometimes on intuition, sometimes on imaginative leaps, as in poetry, that connect together, and thereby clarify hidden, obscure parts of truth.

Now, this is very close to mysticism. It has a kinship to the Judaism of the Kabbalah. A remarkable book, *Sigmund Freud and the Jewish Mystical Tradition*, by David Bakan, shows us that Freud had the Zohar, the classic Jewish book of mysticism, in his working library, and some of his basic ideas, particularly those in dream interpretation, move along the same lines of thought that are to be found there. Also Freud's use of free association is prepared for in such Jewish sources.

Freud's analysis of anti-Semitism itself is in the tradition of the Zohar's analysis. David Bakan shows how both the author of the Zohar and Freud trace the hatred of the Jews to the idea that the Jew-hater, deep within himself, is jealous, as he secretly believes that the Jews really are the chosen of God.

Freud wrote:

The deeper motives of anti-Semitism have their roots in times long past; they come from the unconscious, and I am quite prepared to hear that what I am going to say will at first appear incredible. I venture to assert that the jealousy which the Jews evoked in other peoples by maintaining that they were the first-born, the favourite child of God the Father, has not yet been overcome by those others, just as if the latter had given credence to the assumption.

And, says Bakan, "this 'incredible' theory of anti-Semitism" is set out in the *Zohar* as follows:

And it is because God holds Israel in affection and draws them near to Himself that all the idolatrous nations hate Israel; for they see themselves kept at a distance whilst Israel are brought near. Similarly it was by reason of the love that Jacob showed toward Joseph above all his other sons that they conspired to slay him, though he was their own brother. How much greater, then, must be the enmity of the idolatrous nations toward Israel! . . .

The "other" side of Freud

Bakan goes on to show that Freud in his writings often identified himself with Joseph, the dream-interpreter.

Yet the very last book Freud wrote is often given as an example, in antireligious arguments, to show that in the end this great Jew tried to destroy the very basis of Judaism. The "other" side of Freud appears in a book called *Moses and Monotheism*, written when he was quite an old man. It was begun in Vienna when he was in constant danger from the Nazis, and finished in England after his escape.

Moses and Monotheism is in a way a scholar's game, an attempt from a few hints and guesses, to show that Moses was not really a Jew but an Egyptian. Freud argues that this Egyptian nobleman had developed the idea of One God from the belief in the Sun God, and that he led the Jews out because he needed a people to whom he could teach his religious idea. One intriguing factor remains: it is still the Jews who are chosen—in this way twice chosen—to receive God's word and carry it into history.

But people cried, "There! Freud even took Moses away from the Jews! He made Moses an Egyptian!"

When we examine this, we find it is again an example of the Other. It is an example of search and speculation, of following out even the most negative line of thought, in order to seek further hints of the unknown.

Temptations to self-hatred

There is still a further significance to this fantastic Moses theory, one that Freud was quite hesitant to publish. It shows the existence in Freud himself of another side of Jewishness, a negative side, a Jewish self-hatred such as he had many times uncovered in his patients. It is the deeply buried and often disguised part of ourselves, our own anti-Semitism, coming from world anti-Semitism. For we do hate that aspect of ourselves, the Jewishness that has brought us suffering, even though we also value it most highly. We can't help feeling, thinking, in one way or another, "If I were not a Jew, I wouldn't have to stand for this." Wondering whether it will be difficult to get a job in the banking world, or whether certain influential social circles will be closed to you, or even having to worry about dual loyalty.

We have had evidence of self-hatred pointed out to us in many novels about American Jews. Sometimes it takes the form of jokes about the Jewish mother, or jokes about ultra-kosher Jews; sometimes it takes the form of anti-Zionism, or of believing a Jew should devote himself entirely to the revolutionary cause even if the particular "revolutionary" organization in question is against Judaism.

And so here was a great man like Freud, who remembered, in one of his efforts at self-analysis a revealing incident from his past. As a child, he had resented his father because one day when they were walking together his father had stepped unprotestingly off the sidewalk when some brash young hooligans yelled an insulting Jew-cry at him. Later in his life Freud realized that a germ of Jewish self-hatred had then entered his soul, and when he was a very old man it came out in a fantasy that questioned the Jewishness of father Moses himself!

This was the Other in us, raising his insistent cry, If you don't reveal your whole truth to me, the entire secret of the universe, then I will even deny your existence!

It is an impulse which is both precious and dangerous.

Extreme mysticism

The most intense of our mystics are the ones who try, one might say, to force their way into the Divine consciousness by every extreme, by prolonged fasting, or the opposite way, by wild pleasure-seeking. Some become saintly figures, *Tzaddikim*, yet others, like the false messiah Jacob Frank, end in destructive sin. They cry out that they must reach the lowest depth of evil in order to immerse their souls in every human degradation, so as to "know." Some, like Shabbetai Zvi, become converts to another religion, denying Judaism. And yet all these unfortunate effects of extreme mysticism are of far less importance than the positive effects, the revelations, the release of pure and sincere goodness in multitudes of people, and even the profound sense, in mystics like the Baal Shem Tov, of a personal communication with the Divine Will.

Understanding the "Other"

A touch of the contrary spirit, the questioning spirit, the Other, is necessary in each of us and to Judaism as a whole. But we must be aware of the nature of this impulse. We must not allow ourselves to be led to confuse the Other, who is really part of us, and who remains in the community, with the enemy, the destroyer, who is outside.

Epilogue: A lasting heritage

It is commonly felt that in religion everything has been decided for you. In Judaism, little has been decided for you. For the essence of man, the most painful and most glorious condition of his being, is that he has been endowed with choice. He must even *choose* to obey the Commandments that are his life. Choose—this is the thunderous word that is the condition behind all the commandments and all the laws and all our accumulated wisdom:

I have set before you the knowledge of right and wrong, life and death—choose life.

Choosing our course

Every divinely inspired commandment, every law made by man to implement it, stands as a measuring rod against which a man may test his choices before each act of his life. Then he must choose his course in the light of the Torah. We are told what is good. It is up to us to recognize it and then to act upon it.

Choice in human affairs must sometimes be made when neither course seems ideal for all concerned. Then we may turn to the experience of the past to seek out what is our wisest and highest sense of right. And we have a rich store of advice from Jewish thinkers throughout the ages. Judaism is largely a system of advice, often advice on both sides, wrought out of the longest continuous experience in man's record, out of the most passionate effort to know God. Working from this experience we can be helped to choose in a given case.

Determining our beliefs

In matters of religious belief we must choose in areas where there remains total uncertainty. When discussing the question of life after death, we saw that there are many and various possibilities of belief; some believe in bodily resurrection on earth, some believe in reincarnation in another body, some believe in the continued existence of the soul in a form unknown, and some believe in the finality of death, and our continued existence only through the continuum of life, through our descendants, through the effect, great or small, of our deeds in life on the whole stream of existence.

The desire for continuance

All these ideas center on the feeling of continuation, the desire for a share in immortality, for an expansion of our all too brief time of life.

But time reaches backward as well as forward. It is this impulse, this need, that makes people seek out the record of their ancestry. Particularly is this true now in America, where immigrants arrived, for a great part, with the desire to cut themselves off from their oppression-ridden past. A new society, even a new race of men, was to be created. They wanted their children to have "a different life." Yet very soon, a fearsome sense of nakedness and aloneness began to grow in the land, a sense of "loneliness in the crowd." For many, the link with the past had been destroyed, the sense of a life experience that was longer than one's own time on earth was cut off, and with this came a frantic effort to live totally within one span of life. As a result of this, the sense of immortality both in the past and in eternity was weakened.

We Jews in America were to an extent caught up in this fever. Many Jews hardly knew the name of the *shtetl* their parents had come from, and few could go back in the family history beyond their grandparents. This became an accepted attitude. But with another and then another generation, the need for the immortal link reappeared and grew stronger.

Jewish identity

We have the example of that human need already before us in the Bible. We have the example in those boring lists which are the first things children mock when they begin to study the Bible. The begats. But in memorizing these lists and making their children repeat them, until the time came when they could be written down, our ancients were conserving that backward-flowing part of their immortality, and with it, the wisdom and striving for knowledge of God that was in their strain.

Yet even in this flow, there is a choice. Each man can choose whether he will continue, or will cut himself off from his forebears. The impulse to cut off, to go it alone, to explore other, strange ways of life is strong in us.

It can lead to good, our long experience has shown us, when we do not cut off entirely, but explore, with a home base. This wisdom was imparted to us by the sage, Hillel, in a saying to which he gave prime importance: "Separate not thyself from the community." And from far far back, separation is taught us as the greatest of punishments, for when Cain murdered Abel, it was banishment, and not death, that was God's punishment.

Where did Cain go? There are legends. But he is lost to history, lost to immortality, except for his moment of envy and brutality when he killed his brother and became an eternal example of man making a wrong choice.

Freedom—for what?

But freedom of choice, in the open society of today, particularly here in America, is taken by many people who come from all faiths, largely Christians, as well as Jews, to mean a freedom of unbelief, to mean entering into a vague, agnostic, unstructured life. Somewhere along the line such free

Banks of machines in control towers, like this one at the Wichita, Kansas airport, help man guide planes in safety and avoid collisions. Man still needs higher guidance in controlling the relations of person to person, race to race, nation to nation.

spirits feel terribly empty, spiritually, and they begin to explore all sorts of answers, some of them exotic. In recent times young people have made fads out of one or another of the Far Eastern philosophies, they have sought for gurus, they have tried the passive life of wanting nothing, they have pretended to adopt American Indian cults, they have tried to explode or enlarge their perceptions through drug-taking. But also quite a few of our best young thinkers have chosen a return to a strong, traditional Judaism, called neo-Orthodoxy.

Judaism and social action

Others felt that social action was what they needed to express their spiritual needs. Young Jews have always been prominent in such movements, from the prerevolutionary days in Germany and Russia onward. Moses Hess, an early associate of Karl Marx, broke with his "movement" precisely because he rediscovered his Jewish ethos. In his book *Rome and Jerusalem*, long before the organized Zionist movement, he argued in favor of the Zionist idea.

Many reformists and social revolutionaries carried out their social actions as Jews, working through a Jewish community structure. Some renounced Judaism. Which were the more productive of human good, which were the more satisfied with their lives, would be difficult for us to judge. Only, we do know that Judaism has not been disintegrated, or lost, through this century of social revolution, but that it has on the contrary continued into the inspiring realization of prophecy in the return to Israel, and that Jewish wisdom has flowered in all areas of life.

Again it is the Jewish example that has inspired other nations to seek their identity and their freedom. The first slave revolt in all history was the revolt of the Hebrews in Egypt, and to this day in America it has provided the symbols and the freedom cries of the oppressed. Young Jews went out to help the Negroes in their revolutionary struggle for equal rights, and, in the deep South, a few were even slain. Social action is not a departure from Judaism. It is a fulfillment of it.

If, then, a Jew finds fulfillment in such action, if he works for human betterment in the fight against hunger anywhere on earth, or in the fight for human rights, in a protest organization or in a laboratory or in the government—what further need does he have for Jewishness? This is the question often posed to young people by activists, particularly in the colleges.

Suppose you are going through a period when formal attendance at any kind of religious service seems needless to you, even irksome, and suppose you feel you have found a cause that fulfills all these fine social precepts—what more do you need?

A basis for choice and decisions

You need some system of thought, or belief, that will help you to make your day-to-day decisions, your choices, in whatever cause that attracts you. And also of course in your personal life.

For you will find that social actions become organized, or structured, along one political line or another. A member of a political party must decide at every point whether he wants to continue with the decision or policies of that party. A member of a revolutionary party is strictly bound, even by contradictions in policy. An adherent to a political philosophy may find that it puts a straitjacket on the tumultuous nature of life.

The Jews who ardently helped the Negro freedom movement were astonished when at a certain point that movement became wildly nationalistic and openly anti-Semitic. Not only each Jew but every person involved then had to choose whether to tolerate the anti-Semitic outbursts as part of "a greater cause" or whether to stop trying to help the movement, or in what ways to try to correct it. In this dilemma a Jew could well look to the words of Abraham Heschel in *Israel, An Echo of Eternity.*

We have a right to demand, "Love thy neighbor as thyself." We have no right to demand "Love thy neighbor and kill thyself." No moral teacher has ever asserted, "If one stands with a knife threatening to kill you, bare your heart for him to murder you." There is no moral justification for self-destruction.

This applies not only to the Jew in face of the Negro conflict, but to the Arab-Jewish situation as well, and yet many young intellectual Jews who subscribe to "New Left" policies automatically, because they are in the conformist trend of "the revolution," let themselves be swept along into just such suicidal contradictions. They have given up their own sense of choice.

The Jewish standard and ethos

Every human being in modern, democratic society, where he is constantly confronted with the duty to make and express his choice on every conceivable question, must also know that many pressures are working on him, so as to manipulate his choice. A left-wing pressure may be just as manipulative as a right-wing pressure. He needs some standard, some philosophy in which he can trust, and through which he can make the clearest examination of issues, and the truest choices.

Quite simply, for the Jew, Judaism stands truest. Perhaps the simplest explanation for this is the depth of time and the continuous effort to learn and know the truth, beyond man, through God, that has gone into Judaism, and that aids our choice. A Jew feels himself not as a little man limited by his span of years but as a man who goes far into the past and infinitely into the future, on the same beam of light.

He can refer to the Jewish ethos, to the enlarged sense of what is right and what is wrong, without feeling that he must strictly obey his union faction or his campus clique on the tactic of the moment.

We all know that there is a great danger in our modern machine-made society of being swayed by imperceptible propaganda. Even the person who wants to act for the good of all mankind is in constant danger of having his judgments influenced or formed for him by the overwhelming factor called mass communication. It is difficult for him to thread out, from the constant repetition of radio, television, and the press, what is the proportion of truth. Those who are determined to find the truth on both sides and in its true proportions, on any problem, become a minority. But they are the most necessary of all minorities, and their quest is the most exciting of all human quests.

Rabbi Eugene Borowitz has said, in *How Can a Jew Speak of Faith Today:*

Religion remains the one hope for creating a sizable enough minority of men to keep a technological society moral. It can do so not by avidly compromising but . . . precisely by affirming its faith in a transcendental order of being that grounds and guides man, yet gives him his freedom and demands that he use it for ethical ends.

Abraham Heschel puts it:

. . . the ultimate concern of the Jew is not personal salvation but universal redemption. Redemption is not an event that will take place all at once at the end of days, but a process that goes on all the time. . . . One must live as if the redemption of all men depended on the devotion of one's own life. Thus life, every life, we regard as an immense opportunity to enhance the good that God has placed in His creation. And the vision of a world free of hatred and war, of a world filled with understanding for God as the ocean is filled with water, the certainty of ultimate redemption, must continue to inspire our thought and action.

. . . What man does in his concrete, physical existence is directly relevant to the divine. Man is body and soul and his goal is so to live that both "his heart and his flesh should sing to the living God" (Ps. 84:3). While the soul without the body is a ghost, the body without the soul is a corpse."

Challenges of today

In the need for keeping a technological society moral, not only the Jews but all mankind are faced with major challenges to which traditional religious values may still prove the best—if not the only—solution. Even in the economic realm, thinkers and historians have pointed out that something beyond self-interest is called for. Max Weber among others, has stressed the fact that no economic system can successfully operate on the profit motive alone. "Labor must on the contrary be performed as if it were an absolute end in itself, a calling."

In the political realm, we have said that the Jews were the chief victims of the holocaust. And that is true in point of the percentage of population lost—and in the singular fact that the Jews were victims of a government under which they themselves held citizenship. At the same time, civilian losses in other nations victimized by Nazi assault ran staggeringly high—twelve million in the Soviet alone. And the Nazi attack on Judaism inevitably culminated in an attack on Christianity and Christian churches as being of Jewish origin—that is, as representing standards that constituted a rebuke to Nazi vainglory and brutality.

"Thou shalt have no other gods before Me" rebukes personality worship. "Love thy neighbor as thyself" rebukes racism. "Honor God" rebukes the materialist's claim that violence is necessary to "glory." Jewish respect for individual identity, Jewish stress on individual choice, stand as a bulwark against ignorant and brutal mob-mindedness.

Indeed, Jewish emphasis on sobriety rebukes the contagion of mob-mindedness that produces what Kenneth Clark (referring to certain phases of the French Revolution) has called "communal sadism."

The Jewish ethos comes to the Jew through the whole stream of Jewish experience, basically religious. On balance, this ethos has proven, and remains creative in the life of the individual, and in the universal stream. Is it not, then, a part of our very being, a part which is never to be denied, never to be amputated?

A Jewish soul

Our folk literature uses the expression *Yiddishe neshomeh*, a Jewish soul. Plainly and unabashedly, that is what we feel we are endowed with. Someone who is compassionate, even a little sentimental toward those who are awake, alive and zealous, someone who is eager to share life-discovery, such a person has a *Yiddishe neshomeh*. That Jewish soul has certain responses, all its own. We may call them historically derived. We may call them culturally derived. We may speak in mystical terms of each soul being a spark of the Over-Soul, of the long Jewish consciousness of a compact with God, but beyond definition, this is something we all feel, and we must look to our feelings as well as our reason. We feel the total Jewish experience of life. We feel the experience of Auschwitz and the experience of Israel, as a shared experience of the Jewish soul. We cannot expel this. We must honor the Jewish experience and join it to our personal experience of life, for nothing more profound or revealing, both for darkness and for light, has happened on earth in our time.

The great soul is the soul that has encompassed the furthest extremes, the darkest extremes of the nature of man, as well as the brightest, the deepest torture and the highest elation, and the Jew finds these extremes in what he shares as a Jew. That is why each of us says at Passover, "This is because of what happened to *me,* when *I* came out of Egypt."

We are not the only ones to have a collective yet individual experience. Close to our own is the Negro experience, and perhaps that is why the Negroes have adopted the word "soul." Each people can offer the contents of what it has lived through to all others, but only the people itself can completely feel its experience, just as each individual person is the sole possessor of his own life.

From the most primitive beginning with a stone altar, man has sought to unite himself to what is beyond him, has begged for "a sign." It may even be said that those Jews who have tried to live without any such signs, or rituals, even the "godless" pioneers who established *kibbutzim* in Israel, and the "secular" Jews in America who are unattached to the community and nonobservant, find themselves moved, and yearning for a way to join in reverence, during the two great seasons of festival, the season of awe that comes before winter, and the season of release, in spring.

"Come ye, and let us go up to the mountain of the Lord" (Isaiah 2:3). Passover pilgrims ascend Mount Zion at the call of the shofar as in ancient days. And men still strive to raise their thoughts and lives to the ethical and moral standards set by God.

On the Day of Atonement in Israel, all falls still, as though the entire land were a single soul awaiting the Word of Creation. The most "godless" and the most pious share an utterly mysterious and profound sense of the presence everywhere of the God who has told us what is right and what is good. On the eve of Passover, again, even the most unobservant feel that they must somewhere take part in a Seder.

The abiding guidance of God

So too, in what may be sensed as a community of Jewish souls, we feel this in America. We need not scornfully dismiss the minimal Jews, the once-a-year or twice-a-year Jews, for in the seasons of awe they are drawn by a part of their being that is deeper than their sophistication. How much more satisfying, then, how much more natural, to freely make use, in every day and every moment, of the guidance, and wisdom, and presence of God, in our past, in our Torah, in the timelessness of continuing history, always there for us. How much more satisfying to search and to find, each for his own measure, the form of observance, the form of Jewish life and action, that is his own.

In these pages we have touched on some of these forms, on some of the great and fascinating examples, teachings, treasures, in our long experience. Yet this too is only a prelude, a condensation, scarcely more than what one can absorb while standing on one foot. It is only when one has gone through the basic lessons that one is free for a whole lifetime of learning.

page 14: *National Audubon Society (Grant Haist photo)*; page 16: *Edinburgh University Library*; page 21: *The Bettman Archive, Inc., N.Y.C.*; page 24: *Israel Government Tourist Office*; page 33: *The Oriental Institute of the University of Chicago*; page 37: *Jewish Museum, N.Y.C. (Frank J. Darmstaedter, photographer)*; page 40: *Israel Office of Information, N.Y.C.*; page 51: *American Friends of the Hebrew University, N.Y.C.*; page 55: *Israel Government Tourist Office*; page 59: *Israel Government Press Office, Jerusalem*; page 63: *H. Roger Viollet, Paris*; page 65: *The Museum of Modern Art, N.Y.C. (Alfred Stieglitz photo)*; page 68: *Hebrew Union College–Jewish Institute of Religion, Publicity Department*; page 74: *Israel Office of Information, N.Y.C.*; page 84: *Wide World Photos*; page 90: *Jewish Museum, N.Y.C. (Frank J. Darmstaedter, photographer)*; page 93: *Jewish National Fund*; page 95: *Pierpont Morgan Library, N.Y.C.*; page 96: *Jon Naar, N.Y.C.*; page 99: *Ewing Galloway, N.Y.C.*; page 101: *Yiddish Scientific Institute (YIVO)*; page 106: *Israel Government Information Service, Jerusalem*; page 114: *Wide World Photos*; page 116: *Israel Ministry for Foreign Affairs, Jerusalem*; page 118: *United Nations*; page 122: *Pierpont Morgan Library, N.Y.C.*; page 127: *National Gallery of Art, Washington, D.C. (Andrew Mellon Collection)*; page 133: *H. Roger Viollet, Paris*; page 135: *Liselotte Stein (Fred Stein photo)*; page 141: *Amalgamated Clothing Workers of America*; page 143: *Union of American Hebrew Congregations*; page 146: *The Matson Photo Service, Los Angeles*; page 151: *United Press International, Inc.*; page 153: *Israel Office of Information, N.Y.C.*; page 159: *Joint Distribution Committee*; page 162: *Jewish Museum, N.Y.C. (Frank J. Darmstaedter, photographer)*; pages 166 and 171: *Yiddish Scientific Institute (YIVO)*; page 177: *Zionist Archives and Library, N.Y.C.*; page 182: *The Bettmann Archive, Inc., N.Y.C.*; page 187: *Israel Office of Information, N.Y.C.*

Index

TEMPLE BETH SHOLOM
P.O. BOX 445
STRATFORD, CT 06497